Wake-Up Calls

Joan Lunden

McGraw-Hill

New York St. Louis San Francisco Washington, D.C. Auckland
Bogotá Caracas Lisbon London Madrid Mexico City Milan
Montreal New Delhi San Juan Singapore Sydney Tokyo Toronto

McGraw-Hill

A Division of The McGraw·Hill Companies

1234567890 WCTWCT 09876543210

ISBN 0-07-136126-X

Printed and bound by Quebecor World Taunton.

McGraw-Hill books are available at special quantity discounts to use as
premiums and sales promotions, or for use in corporate training programs.
For more information, please write to the Director of Special Sales,
Professional Publishing, McGraw-Hill, Two Penn Plaza, New York, NY
10121-2298. Or contact your local bookstore.

❸ This book is printed on recycled, acid-free paper containing a minimum
of 50% recycled, de-inked fiber.

CONTENTS

DEDICATION

*M*y life has been so greatly influenced and enhanced by the words and thoughts of others writers—those who have pondered our purpose, searched for the secrets of success and happiness, and reminded us of our human weaknesses.

For instance, as I began reading books by Deepak Chopra the way I looked at life and its possibilities changed. From "Ageless Body, Timeless Mind", I learned that I could alter my biology by altering my thinking, and my world opened up. I'll never forget the first time I read Jonathan Kabat-Zinn's *Wherever You Go, There You Are*, which reminded me that my life is not that which happens to me, but, instead, is my interpretation of what's happening. I quickly became more cognizant of those glasses through which I saw the world—and how they affected my joy and happiness. Brian Luke Seaward's *Stand Like Mountain, Flow Like Water*, helped me devise strategies for coping with life's changes and stresses. And my good friend and colleague Dr. Ellen McGrath has been there to help me personally navigate my opportunities and challenges. And then, for "over the top" motivation to get to the top, I've been fortunate enough to have experienced first-hand Tony Robbins and Zig Ziglar, two of the greatest motivators. I have been fascinated by the power all of these people have to empower others, and they have challenged me to attempt it myself. For their inspiration, I thank them all.

On a personal level, I consider myself most fortunate to have found people who believe in me and my projects, and who've worked hard to help me realize my dreams. Marc Chamlin has been more than my attorney, he has been a trusted friend— always there with my best interest at heart. I know I can test new waters with Marc watching my back. Meanwhile, always watching my pocketbook are Richard Koenigsberg and David Harris. They have not only made my money grow but have empowered me to have a sense of control of my finances. I also thank Marc for introducing me to Al Lowman, who became my book agent. As an ardent believer in the power of enthusiasm, I have used Al's passionate enthusiasm for my books as a motivation to keep writing.

And of course, a special thanks to my editor Nancy Mikhail for believing in this concept, Arlene Lee for adding her artistic touch, editor Mary Glenn for seeing it through to its finish, Claudia Boutote for her promotional efforts, and to Peter McCurdy and everyone else at McGraw-Hill for their support and dedication to this book. Thanks, too, to Lynn Goldberg,

Camille McDuffy, and Grace McQuade for their strategic publicity plans.

A life that generates enough stories to fill a book usually comes with a busy schedule filled with responsibilities—and the challenge to juggle everything with aplomb. Behind every successful person who is out there touching other lives are dedicated people who work endlessly for the cause yet never receive public adulation or recognition. To me, Jill Seigerman is the epitome of this selfless hard worker. For her class, her calmness, and the enthusiasm she brought to her work, I thank her from the bottom of my heart. I wish her happiness in her new role, as mommy to little Alexandra Ray. And just when I might have panicked at the thought of this change, I found a new partner in Lori Bzura. Jill left big shoes to fill—but Lori has brought the same calm, and class, and work ethic to the job. Another dedicated selfless worker who also looks to do not only what is required, but a little more. I admire this kind of desire to always strive to challenge oneself, and to grow.

As for my family, the essence of this book can certainly be traced back to my childhood. Kudos to my spirited mom, known to her friends as Glitzy Glady, for planting that seed of enthusiasm and determination in me.

And a very special thanks to my three fabulous daughters, Jamie, Lindsay, and Sarah for being my Buddha task-masters, challenging me daily to hold on to my patience, teaching me to let go of my stresses, and giving me so many reasons to smile. By teaching them to be grateful for our wonderful lives, I am reminded to do the same. If I am a good role model for them, and can help guide them to lead happy productive lives, then I will have succeeded in my most important role. I am filled with excitement and pride when I see the people they are becoming.

And finally, thank you to my wonderful, loving, supportive husband Jeff, for being the ultimate wake-up call in my life. As Babe Ruth said, "It ain't over 'til it's over." But damn, to get a sequel this exciting and romantic is more than I ever could have hoped for. If I ever doubted that we have the power to make choices, to give our lives new direction, he has certainly proven otherwise—that the best *is* yet to come.

Wake-Up Calls

INTRODUCTION

A Mind Lift Is Better Than a Face Lift!

In the absence of wake-up calls,
many of us never really confront the critical issues of life.
—Stephen Covey, *First Things First*

We have all come to accept that if we want fit, well-toned bodies and strong muscles, we must exercise. But what about our "inner" strength? How do you build courage, grace, dignity, self-esteem, and positive thinking? These inner "spiritual" muscles need to be strengthened as well so we can call upon them in challenging times and dare to dream and to risk in order to achieve success and personal happiness.

For too many of us, life often feels like a struggle. At those times, we could all use some inspiration, encouragement, and words of hope. We could all benefit from learning how to reduce our stresses, to let go of our emotional blocks, and to embrace life's joy. We could all use a reminder to feel gratitude for what we have, rather than anxiety over what we don't have.

There is only one corner of the universe you can be certain of improving, and that's your own self.
—*Aldous Huxley*

Yesterday's the past, tomorrow's the future, today is a gift. That's why they call it the present.
—*Unknown*

A misty morning does not signify a cloudy day.
—*An ancient proverb*

For this, I've always been drawn to motivational and inspirational books. I find that they not only give me guidance but also challenge me to be a better person and to act on my dreams. For years, I've collected my favorite quotes, and I often refer to them. They brighten my spirits, calm my anxieties, and help me to let go of my unrealistic expectations. In fact, I've come to find that no matter how stressful my day—a little coaching from my collection of quotes can always help give me a confidence boost—that spark of radiance that shines from within.

A single sunbeam is enough to drive away any shadows.
—Saint Francis of Assisi

We can all learn to live jubilantly. We can all learn to alter our attitudes so that we can better realize our dreams. We can all end negative thinking that weighs down our self-esteem and colors our view of life. We can all start down the road to self-improvement at any point in our lives. It does take work, but negative thinking is a habit that can be broken.

The journey of a thousand miles starts with a single step.
—Lao-Tzu

**All experience is a torch
to light the way of each new challenge.**
—*Unknown*

Life is like a 10-speed bike. We all have gears we never use.
—*Charles Schultz*

I say we bust out of the brain bondage that drains our energy and short circuits our happiness. A few small attitude adjustments—call them mental makeovers—can make a huge difference in your life. I know they have in mine.

**You know—life's a real bumpy road,
what you've got to develop are good shock absorbers.**
Uncle Charlie, My Three Sons

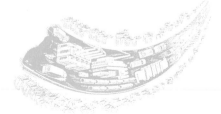

In one of my favorite inspirational books, I read a quote by Toni Morrison that said, "If there's a book you really want to read, but it hasn't been written yet, then you must write it." Thank you, Toni, for the motivation to help me undertake this project. I hope this book encourages people to nurture their minds with great thoughts. I know, for me, it has become a great passion.

We all live in suspense from day to day, from hour to hour, in other words, we are the hero of our own story.
—*Mary McCarthy*

They say you teach best what you most need to know. And so I share with you some winning strategies that have worked for me, particularly this thought by W. Clement Stone on the difference between a novel and a self-help book. "In a novel, the author writes the conclusion; in a self-help book, the reader writes the conclusion by the action they take."

Joan Lunden

Attitudes Are Contagious— Is Yours Worth Catching?

*You've got to get up every morning with determination
if you're going to go to bed with satisfaction.*
—George Horace Lorimer

It seems that no matter how much you reflect, meditate, eat right, and breathe deeply...from time to time you still wake up on the wrong side of the bed! Do you have mornings where you just feel *out of sorts?*

I know I've had mornings like that—and sometimes for no good reason. When I was hosting "Good Morning America," this was, of course, a much bigger problem for me. One of our stage directors, Patty Sheenan, always sensed when Charlie Gibson or I was having a tough morning. That was when she would look us square in the eye and say, "You can start your day over at any time." I always appreciated that gentle reminder. It's

FACING PAGE: Summer 2000—It was only my attitude and determination that got me to the top of Camp Takajo's 50 foot climbing wall.

reassuring to know that I can control how I feel and what I do on any given day. The way I choose to see the world creates the world I see.

Your living is determined not so much by what life brings to you...as by the attitude you bring to life.
—*John Homer Mills*

The good news is, that the bad news can be turned into good news when you change your attitude.
—*Robert Schuller*

An optimist sees an opportunity in every calamity; a pessimist sees a calamity in every opportunity.
—*Sir Winston Churchill*

Positive thoughts are extremely powerful. It was no accident that I started writing this book with a chapter on positive thinking. I've interviewed many writers over the years who have shared their thoughts on the misery of "writer's block." While empathetic, I now realize that you can't really know what a person is going through until you have experienced the same situation. Now I was questioning whether or not I could inspire others. Could I possibly even make someone laugh? I needed positive reinforcement to put me on the right track:

DOUBT:	POSITIVE REINFORCEMENT:
Who am I to write a book?	Today, I have something to contribute.
These quotes move me, will others care?	Today, I have the opportunity to share my thoughts with with others.
How do I share the chaos called my life?	Today, I find the humor in the emotional experience called life.
Will this book make a difference?	Today, I let go of my insecurities and trust in my abilities.
How long will I have to stare at this blank page?	Today, I will commit to filling a page (even if I throw it out tomorrow).

Ok, now I feel better....Everything we think affects our spirit, our attitude, and our ability to participate in life. In fact, it has often been said that *what we become is what we think about most of the time.*

There is no danger of developing eye strain from
looking on the bright side of things.

—*Unknown*

The greater part of our happiness or misery depends
on our dispositions and not on our circumstances.

—*Martha Washington*

Some people look at the world and say "why?"
Some people look at the world and say "why not?"

—*George Bernard Shaw*

We need to pay close attention to the menu of thoughts and
images that runs through our minds. If we choose positive
thoughts and images, they then become our inspirations.
Conversely, negative thoughts become our demons, our tormen-
tors, and our roadblocks.

Two men looked out through prison bars;
one saw mud, the other, stars.

—*James Allen*

**Nothing can stop the man with the
right mental attitude from achieving his goal: nothing on
earth can help the man with the wrong mental attitude.**
—*Thomas Jefferson*

**Life is ten percent what you make it, and
ninety percent how you take it.**
—*Irving Berlin*

I've come to think of a positive attitude as an "inside job." Just as we nurture our physical bodies with the right vitamins and nutrients, we must nurture our minds with good thoughts. I know that there are certain songs that can instantly put me in a positive frame of mind. I keep a Carole King CD in my car at all times, just so I can turn up the volume to hear "You've got to get up every morning with a smile on your face, and show the world all the love in your heart. Then people gonna treat you better. You're gonna find, yes, you will, that you're beautiful as you feel." This is my sure-fire way of putting a smile on my face—it works every time!

The Art of Putting a Spring in Your Step...

1. Stretch—I like waking up my body and stretching my muscles to get my blood flowing and my body moving.

2. Sit-ups and butt lifts—While I'm waiting for the shower to warm up, I get down on the floor and do a series of abdominal and glute exercises to tone my body and reinforce my posture for the day.

3. Water—Drink plenty of water! Dehydration is a key cause of fatigue. Water helps maintain your blood pressure and your body temperature. I try to drink at least 6 to 8 eight-ounce glasses of water daily.

4. Music—Let the music move you! I find that nothing gets me going faster than music with a beat that won't let me sit still. In fact, if I'm in a sluggish mood, I can change my mood with music. I put on Sheryl Crow's "All I Wanna Do Is Have Some Fun" or Gloria Estefan's "Rhythm Is Gonna Get Ya."

5. Smile—The physical act of smiling has an effect on the rest of your body. It almost gives your body a cue to be happy. I never leave my dressing room before a show without flashing my pearly whites. It sets my mood for the day.

We are the only creatures on earth who
can change our biology by what we think and feel.
—*Deepak Chopra*

Tomorrow is the most important thing in life.
Comes into us at midnight very clean. It's perfect when it
arrives and it puts itself in our hands.
It hopes we've learned something from yesterday.
—*John Wayne*

I was once asked what makes one television broadcaster better than another. And I think my answer would hold true for almost any area of life, and that answer is *enthusiasm*. We can listen to a myriad of experts with the same information, but it is the one who is truly enthusiastic about the information he or she has to deliver—the one whose passion excites our curiosity—with whom we will connect.

I can't imagine a person becoming a success who doesn't
give this game of life everything he's got.
—*Walter Cronkite*

**A successful man is one who can lay a
firm foundation with bricks that others throw at him.**
—*David Brinkley*

I've come to the conclusion that enthusiasm is perhaps the greatest asset anyone can have. It is the key ingredient to success. You can have a wealth of skills, but if your heart is not in it, your work will reflect it. If you have enthusiasm, you will find the energy to acquire the necessary skills and draw to you all the people and support you need to succeed. Enthusiasm beats power, money and influence.

**Don't ever let me catch you singing like that again,
without enthusiasm. You're nothing,
if you aren't excited by what you are doing.**
—*Frank Sinatra* to his son, Frank, Jr.

After I left "Good Morning America," it seems everyone expected me to move to another talk or news show. Would I team up with Bryant Gumbel on CBS's "The Early Show" or with Regis when Kathie Lee left? But as much as I tried to gather my enthusiasm for one of these, the choices were not so obvious to me. I knew all too well what these kinds of commitments meant to one's life. I couldn't seem to get enthusiastic about any of these prospects, even though I felt the pressure to do what everyone expected. My heart told me that that path just wasn't right for me at this point in time. I yearned for some normalcy in my life and for time with my family. I knew my challenge now was to find projects where I could use my talents and earn a living, but not have to sign over my life to a live daily show.

By not succumbing to this pressure, I left myself open to discover new opportunities. Little would I have guessed that this challenge would lead me to the super-market aisles! But earlier this year I was contacted to host a new out-of-home television network that will appear on large screens in supermarkets throughout the country. It's called "The Women's Supermarket Network," and it will disseminate health and wellness news, consumer tips, and light easy recipe ideas to shoppers. How exciting it is to be reunited with my viewers in such a comfortable venue (first on T.V. screens in their bedrooms or kitchens and now once again, on screens in their grocery aisles!)—I now could get enthusiastic about being their shopping companion!

Equally exciting is that I can be in at the ground level of a new project...a project with so much potential. When the company showed me the screens that had been in one supermarket chain for the year-long test, I was bubbling with ideas, recommendations, and even thoughts on why some of the existing programming might not work. I was so enthusiastic—I couldn't help myself. I saw an opportunity to draw upon my 20 years of experience...to not only host—but to program and produce this new television concept. Two days later, Bob Jacobs, the CEO of the company, called my attorney to say he, too, felt my enthusiasm and my understanding of the project, and then he proposed that I become president of "The Women's Supermarket Network"— not just the host!

Did I know exactly how to run a big company? No, but I'm learning, and my enthusiasm for this new venture has been contagious; I've been able to surround myself with a talented group of experienced people to help me launch this innovative project. Since there are always cashflow risks with a new start-up company, I agreed to take a financial ownership position in lieu of a big salary. This is called "betting on yourself" and taking a risk because you believe in the concept—and believe it will be successful. This is something men do all the time in the workplace, but it seems more difficult for women to take these kinds of risks. I believe that good programming with useful information that will save women time, money, or calories will be successful!

᠎᠎᠎

Any fact facing us is not as important as our attitude toward it, for that determines our success or failure.
—*Norman Vincent Peale*

I'm also excited that the A&E Network will now carry my "Behind Closed Doors" specials and has asked me to host "Biography" and other programs. It's such a classy, smart network with such a sterling reputation—I kind of feel like I am back in high school and was just asked to join the Honor Society. It's exciting to be in a workplace that has always kept the bar raised high. What is especially nice and refreshing is that even though there will be budgetary challenges in terms of a cable budget versus a network budget, I will be working for a network that truly appreciates my abilities. Feeling their enthusiasm for my contribution fuels me with new energy and ideas for my programs.

"Behind Closed Doors" at the largest women's maximum security prison, I spent time in solitary confinement and on death row for A&E.

> **Every great and commanding movement in the annals of the world, is the triumph of enthusiasm. Nothing great was ever achieved without it.**
> —*Ralph Waldo Emerson*

Enthusiasm radiates from within people as they walk into a room, ready to pitch an idea or be the life of the party—their body language, their exuberance, their excitement, and their confidence—all make you ready to accept whatever they have to offer. They have the "attitude most likely to succeed."

Don't give up. Keep going.
There is always a chance that you stumble onto
something terrific. I have never heard of anyone stumbling
over anything while he was sitting down.
—Ann Landers

I think and think for months and years. Ninety-nine
times, the conclusion is false. The hundredth time, I am right.
—Albert Einstein

I once read, "Enthusiasm is never an orphan; it multiplies." I know that each morning as I said hello to the nation on "Good Morning America," my enthusiasm for the day was a big part of why people chose to start their day with us. Everyone can develop this kind of winning attitude.

The fact that one's enthusiasm can have such a lasting effect on others is one of the reasons why I enjoy writing, even though it requires so much hard work. Then, of course, every time I say I'm not going to write anymore—that it's just too time consuming—I run into someone who tells me how much one of my books helped them.

My husband Jeff and I walked into a delicatessen the other day and a woman in her 60s approached me. She said a few months earlier she was in the depths of depression, for she had just lost her husband and was having difficulty moving on in her life. She went into a book store to get a book on tape for the two-hour drive to her sister's house. She saw my *A Bend In the Road Is Not the End of the Road*, and she knew me from waking up with me every morning all those years, so she bought it and popped it in her tape player.

She said she had tears streaming down her face, listening to me share my tough times—and that she gained strength in my sharing how I made it around the next bend. The book totally changed her outlook. She said that as soon as she got herself excited about the life she could have ahead—instead of being focused on what she had lost—it was like "taking a happiness drug."

How can I *not* keep doing this?!

The journey in between what you once were and who you are now becoming is where the dance of life really takes place.
—*Barbara De Angelis,* Inspiration About Love

Let me tell you the secret that has led me to my goal. My strength lies solely in my tenacity.
—*Louis Pasteur*

The way you carry yourself into your workplace or into an important meeting can make you look like it's your first day on the job or the CEO. People make decisions about you and your ideas based on what they see—your facial expression, your body language, and your enthusiasm. So if you want to communicate confidence and strength, and sell your idea, start by being enthusiastic. That's why I always say, go to work *before* you go to work!

If you aren't fired with enthusiasm, you will be fired with enthusiasm.
—*Vince Lombardi*

I am glad that I'm an optimist.
The pessimist is half-licked before he starts.
—*Thomas A. Buckner*

If you think you can, you can.
And if you think you can't, you're right.
—*Mary Kay Ash*

Gautama Buddah wrote, "We are what we think. All that we are arises with our thoughts. With our thoughts, we make our world." Even the clichés that may seem so trite sometimes turn out to be so true. For instance, my mom always used to say, "Put on your rose colored glasses." "Every cloud has a silver lining!" Oh, and how could I forget, "Always see the glass half full." Don't you hate it when your mom's always right? Granted, a positive attitude will not solve all of your problems.

However, at the very least, it will annoy enough people to make it worth the effort!

Let *Wake-Up Calls* inspire you to find and hold on to those feelings that put a smile on your face, that help you wake up with a spring in your step. Let the words that follow in these pages motivate you to tackle the day instead of having the day wipe you out. Attitude is everything and I've certainly found over the years that my attitude can even evoke a similar response in others. Attitudes tend to be contagious....Is yours worth catching?

3 STEPS TO MAINTAINING A POSITIVE ATTITUDE:

- ❍ Make a contract with yourself to stay focused on the positive.
- ❍ Attitude Check—Constantly check in with yourself to see if your attitude is worth catching.
- ❍ Always have something to look forward to Enthusiasm = Energy. Create exciting momentum in your life.

The most handicapped person
in the world is a negative thinker.
—*Unknown*

The mind is like a parachute. It works best when it is open.
—*Unknown*

My philosophy is that not only are you responsible
for your life, but doing the best at this moment puts you in
the best place for the next moment.
—*Oprah Winfrey*

How Can You Stuff a Big Life into a Small Dream?

Shoot for the moon.
Even if you miss, you land among the stars.
—Les Brown

Growing up, my mom used to encourage me to "always have something to look forward to." Over the years, I have found that having plans and goals has helped me to keep moving forward. As I achieve goals, it gives me a sense of accomplishment and courage to set new ones.

In the beginning, I was timid about setting big goals, but I've found that we only hit at those things we aim at, so we better aim at something high. Babe Ruth said it this way, "Never let the fear of striking out get in your way."

At Spring Training with the Chicago Cubs.

FACING PAGE: After my first F-18 landing on the USS Eisenhower.

I've always tried to apply Babe's philosophy to life. Just as he would swing hard, we can set goals for ourselves with the same enthusiasm.

Setting goals is one of the most powerful ways to create the life you really want. People with goals succeed because they know where they are going.

Destiny is not a matter of chance; it is a matter of choice. It is not a thing to be waited for: it is a thing to be achieved.
—William Jennings Bryan

Everything starts with yourself—with you making up your mind about what you're going to do with your life.
—Tony Dorsett

Far away there in the sunshine are my highest aspirations. I may not reach them, but I can look up and see their beauty, believe in them, and try to follow where they lead.
—Louisa May Alcott

The act of defining our dreams and goals and actually writing them down—both short term and long term, is very effective. Setting short-term goals keeps us focused on what we need to accomplish and hopefully include in our daily lives. What should you add to your list? Maybe you want to start taking better care of yourself, have more quality time with your children, or put the spark back in your marriage. Add them to your list. Put these on your "to do" list and you will be reminded of those things you really want in your life.

**Make a list of all the things you believed in before
you were told they were impossible.**
—*Unknown*

**Use what talents you possess. The woods would be very silent
if no birds sang there except those that sang best.**
—*Henry Van Dyke*

I remember how vulnerable I felt when I left "Good Morning America." Let's be honest, I was a single mom with three children to support, and I was letting go of my security blanket. Even though I knew it was time to move on, not knowing what my next move would be was terrifying. I found that going through this process, writing down both short-term and long-term goals, allowed me to feel like I had some control in my life. By defining my short-term goals, I was able to get some breathing space before feeling the pressure to solidify my long-term plans. Just having the structure of a daily, live show lifted from my life was unnerving. My mom's mantra, "Always have something to look forward to" came to mind. So I filled my schedule with speaking engagements, public awareness campaigns, and long-awaited adventure trips, which all kept my life exciting and fulfilling short term. This tactic worked for me, and gave me time to focus more confidently on the long term.

Where are you going? What are you *doing* to get there?

It's a dream until you write it down…then it's a goal.
—*Unknown*

**You must begin to think of
yourself as becoming the person you want to be.**
—*David Viscott*

**If you have built castles in the air,
your work need not be lost; that is where they should be.
Now put the foundations under them.**
—*Henry David Thoreau*

What would you like to add to your "to do" list?

- Enroll in that class you always wanted to take?
- Organize your finances?
- Get rid of the clutter at the office, in your home, in your mind?
- Rediscover a sense of play with your children?
- Do charity work?
- Reconcile with a family member or old friend?
- Travel to exotic places?
- Open a business?

OK, now take the time to acknowledge your dreams and desires, and write them down. As you begin to make your list of short and long term goals, dare to add them to your "to-do list."

It's important to identify our goals and dreams. Did you see the movie, *Out of Africa?* My favorite line from the film went something like this: "My biggest fear was that I would come to the end of my life, and discover that I lived someone else's dream." How many people live their lives, and die, never recognizing their dreams or acting on them, while others seize every opportunity to enjoy their potential? Even if you can't realize some of your goals, identifying them helps us understand what we hope to achieve, what we have to offer, and, ultimately, what our dreams are.

Take care to do what you like or
you will be forced to like what you do.
—*George Bernard Shaw*

The future belongs to those who
believe in the beauty of their dreams.
—*Eleanor Roosevelt*

The greater danger for most of us is not that our aim is
too high and we miss it, but that it is too low and we reach it.
—*Michelangelo*

For the last few years, I've kept a "dream journal." Whenever I
get an idea for a book, a television show, a clothing line, or a day
spa (come on, it's a *dream* journal!), I write
about it in this little notebook I keep
by my bed. Sometimes I'll find
that I'll return to my "dream
journal," only to realize that
now I *can* accomplish something that seemed like an
impossible dream when I first
put it on paper. *Wake-Up Calls* is

a great example. I've been collecting inspirational and motivational quotes for years, and have always wanted to share my collection. With that dream in mind, I've diligently continued collecting them until finally the day came when I could achieve this goal.

Dreams are illustrations from the book your soul is writing about you.
—*Marsha Norman*

Life is a great big canvas, and you should throw all the paint on it you can.
—*Danny Kaye*

To accomplish great things, we must not only act, but also dream; not only plan but also believe.
—*Anatole France*

Every now and then you hear of a story that makes such an impression on you that it continues to inspire you. Whenever I get frustrated and think that my dreams are too far out of reach,

I remember the story of one of the greatest leaders of our time. Born into a poor family, his parents were virtually illiterate and, in fact, his own education was limited. He failed in business at the ages of 22 and 24, and had a nervous breakdown at the age of 27. With lofty ambitions to make all people equal, he entered politics, only to be defeated in eight different elections—runs for the Illinois legislature, the U.S. Senate, House of Representatives, speaker, elector, and vice president. In 1861, he was finally elected President of the United States. Have you guessed who I'm talking about yet? Abraham Lincoln—he never gave up his dream of a "government of the people, by the people, and for the people." To me he represents what it means to dream, to persevere, and to never give up.

**Always bear in mind that your own resolution
to succeed is more important than any other thing.**
—Abraham Lincoln

My mantra has become, "Know no boundaries." This does not suggest reckless abandon, but an open mind that asks, "What would I attempt to do if I were sure I wouldn't fail?" Taking away the self-imposed limits that our own insecurities tend to impose, our list can take on a whole new shape.

There is a great deal of unmapped country within us.
—*George Eliot*

Imagination is the highest kite one can fly.
—*Lauren Bacall*

Think of yourself as the CEO of your life. Now that you're in charge, give yourself permission to acknowledge your desires. Use your mind to empower you, not limit you. OK boss, your dreams are now "works in progress." You have taken the first steps toward actualizing them. You can give a dream a life of its own.

**A man's reach should exceed his grasp,
or what's a heaven for?**
—*Robert Browning*

**Dreams are like letters from God.
Isn't it time you answered your mail?**
—*Marie Louis von Franz*

Now it's your turn to proceed as if it were impossible to fail. Franklin Roosevelt once said, "The only limit to our realization of tomorrow will be our doubts of today." How many times have you accomplished something only to think back on that moment when you were so sure you couldn't? I know I've done this, and it makes me shake my head and ask myself, "Why did I agonize over this, because it only made it that much harder?" If only we could remember that all things appear difficult at first. All things are possible…Pass the word!

Life can only disappoint you if you let it.
—*Mark Hopkins*

It is no use to wait for your ship to come in unless you have sent one out.
—*Anonymous*

Adventure is worthwhile in itself.
—*Amelia Earhart*

**One can never consent to creep
when one feels an impulse to soar.**
—*Helen Keller*

10 ways to act on your dreams:

1. Take "what if" out of your vocabulary.
2. Make lists of your dreams and goals.
3. Get going—take at least one step toward
   making it a reality.
4. Look at past successes—assess your strengths.
5. Understand the goal—do the research.
6. Become aware of potential obstacles.
7. Understand the finances involved.
8. Talk to others to get objective opinions.
9. Make a plan—start small—small triumphs will boost
   confidence in order to tackle the big-picture projects.
10. Make the time.

Opportunity dances with those who are
already on the dance floor.

—*H. Jackson Brown Jr.*

The world makes way for the man
who knows where he is going.

—*Ralph Waldo Emerson*

Go Out on a Limb, That's Where the Fruit Is!

Only those that risk going too far
can possibly find out how far one can go.
—T. S. Eliot

We never know what we can do until we try…and courage and tenacity are half the victory. And when you dare to do something you never thought yourself capable of, you feel a rush of glory. However, you know the old saying, "no guts, no glory." Take, for example, when I decided to tackle climbing the Grand Tetons in Wyoming with a group from my gym. I had to muster up all the courage and confidence I could just to get on the bus that would take us there. Day One, the hike to base camp sounded like it would be a piece of cake. However, after hiking only several hundred feet from the parking lot, we encountered snow. By the time we reached our destination (at 8500 feet), we began to suffer the effects of altitude sickness. What did I say about

FACING PAGE: I don't think my treadmill ever hit this incline!

"guts and glory"? I was so busy puking my guts out, the glory of spending the first night on the mountain was somewhat lost! This was clearly an example of something that I had so wanted to believe I could do. But to say that I still wasn't sure I'd make it was the understatement of the year. But the opportunity had presented itself—and I knew I would be conquering more than the mountain. I would be conquering my own fears and self-imposed self-limits. I'll admit it now—even though I was fiercely determined to succeed, I truly didn't believe I would. While I may not have made it to the very highest peak, I learned the definition of a summit: anywhere you stand, from wherever you look, you're looking down. Summits can be different for each of us, but reaching them gives you strength you didn't know you had—especially when you conquer so many fears on your way there.

Sigmund Freud said, "Out of your vulnerabilities will come your strength." It's all about getting up and dancing with whatever life brings us. This builds courage and seeds our confidence to try even more. If we never attempt things beyond what we've already mastered, we'll never grow. Progress almost always involves risks.

You cannot discover new oceans unless
you have the courage to lose sight of the shore.
—*From* Achieve Your Dreams

The greatest mistake you can
make, is to be afraid of making one.
—*Elbert Hubbard*

All adventures, especially into new territory, are scary.
—*Sally Ride,* first American woman astronaut to fly in space

If you risk nothing, then you risk everything.
—*Geena Davis*

Sure risk taking is inherently failure prone. Otherwise, it would be called "sure thing taking." But I've adopted Teddy Roosevelt's philosophy: "Whenever you're asked if you can do something, say 'Yes, yes I can!' Then get busy figuring out how to do it." Sometimes you just have to stick your neck out and have faith.

**There would be nothing to frighten you
if you refused to be afraid.**
—*Mahatma Gandhi*

A turtle travels only when it sticks its neck out.
—*Unknown*

**You may be disappointed if you fail, but
you are doomed if you don't try.**
—*Beverly Sills*

People always seem surprised to learn that, for years, I have had a fear of public speaking. After working in front of a television viewing audience all those years, I guess I can understand why it seems so odd. People would often ask, "How can you be nervous in front of a few hundred people when millions of people saw you every-day?" I've always replied, "But I didn't *see* any of them!"

Speaking in front of a large audience (oh let me be honest—even a small audience) used to unnerve me. Even now, I get a few butterflies, but not like the fear that used to give me a stomach ache—and make me break out in a sweat.

I used to avoid public speaking at any cost. And yet, when I left "Good Morning America," I was fiercely determined to conquer my fear. I'm not sure why it meant so much to me to get over this. I think it's because I realized that I could disseminate important information to people which could affect their lives in a positive, inspiring way. But before I could inspire *anyone*, I had to get comfortable with it myself!

My first few appearances in front of large audiences were almost surreal. I can barely remember stepping out on stage. But I can remember quite vividly looking out at 25,000 people—it was like a human sea. (To be honest, it was like a big wave that looked like it was going to swallow me.) Little by little, I began to feel more comfortable, but I knew that I was still too insecure to be totally relaxed on stage.

Each time I stepped out, I flexed my courage muscle. I've gone through stages—first, just getting over the initial panic—then gaining a comfort level—and finally, truly connecting with the audience. In thinking back, there were some very successful techniques I used to ease my discomfort on stage: (1) Imitating successful behavior—I studied the performances of dynamic speakers. (2) Positive imagery—Like a dress rehearsal, I imagined myself captivating the audience. (3) Relaxation techniques—Breathing, relaxation exercises, and positive self-talk helped calm me. (4) Rehearse with friends who will give you honest feedback. (5) Spoke with experts who could assure me that my information was correct and up to date. (6) Wore my best outfit.

There was one particular speaking engagement that was a real turning point for me. It was a particularly overwhelming time both personally and professionally. Overcommitted and on the road, I was fielding crisis calls from my daughters at home—one had a broken leg and lost her wallet while on vacation, another had just broken up with her boyfriend, and the other one needed help with her term paper. So many layers of my life seemed out of control that, as I walked onto the stage, I used those vulnerabilities as the thread that would tie me to the audience. In doing so, it became a true sharing experience, as opposed to my standard speech. It was an amazing breakthrough. I abandoned the speech I had written, and spent 30 minutes talking to those 25,000 people as if they were close friends. It was arguably the most powerful performance I'd ever given. I remember Tony Robbins, who runs these motivational seminars, saying, "I'm not quite sure what I just witnessed, but something amazing just happened with you on that stage." He saw that I had let go of my fears and vulnerabilities and was therefore able to connect with and empower others.

Decide that you want it more than you are afraid of it.
—*Bill Cosby*

**Courage is the art of being the
only one who knows you're scared to death.**
—*Earl Wilson*

To live is to explore, to reach out and, yes, to take risks. My friends all tease me about my "stupid human tricks" as they call them. Like flying in an F-16 with the Thunderbirds or flying at 70,000 feet in a U2 with the U.S. Air Force, parachuting off a mountain top, or bungee jumping off a bridge. Everyone says, "You're too much," and maybe they're right, but I think they sense the exhilaration that comes from setting your sights high and actually reaching them.

To see what few have seen,
you must go where few have gone.
—*Buddha*

Somehow I can't believe that there are any heights that can't be scaled by a man who knows the secret of making his dreams come true. This special secret, it seems to me, can be summarized in four C's. They are curiosity, confidence, courage and constancy and the greatest of these is confidence. When you believe in a thing, believe in it all the way.
—*Walt Disney*

You too *can* make your life more exciting. You *can* have more. First, you need to ask yourself what it is you want. This may seem obvious, but many people will answer this question with, "I don't know. I just know my life is boring." Well, then, do something about it! Dream! Imagine! As Albert Einstein said, "Imagination is more important than knowledge."

Argue for your limitations and they are yours.
—*Richard Bach*

It's not trespassing when you cross your own boundaries.
—*Unknown*

**Yes, you can be a dreamer and a doer too, if you
will remove one word from your vocabulary: Impossible.**
—*Robert H. Schuller*

**It is not because things are difficult that we do not dare;
it is because we do not dare that they are difficult.**
—*Seneca*

All of this takes courage. I'll never forget the first time I heard, "Courage is like a muscle, it's strengthened by use." Those words became emblazoned in my mind. And each time I conquer another challenge that I wasn't sure I could, I can feel that muscle getting stronger and stronger.

We don't know who we are until we see what we can do.
—*Martha Grimes,* Writer's Handbook

If your life is free of failures,
you're not taking enough risks.
—*Unknown*

When written in Chinese, the word "crisis" is
composed of two characters. One represents danger and
the other represents opportunity.
—*John F. Kennedy*

You can gain strength, courage and confidence, by
every experience in which you really stop to look fear in the
face. You must do the thing you think you cannot do.
—*Eleanor Roosevelt*

I found a great exercise to help us work through our fears and to
strengthen our courage and risk muscles. Make a list of all the
ways you would end this sentence:

"If I were not afraid, I would...."

When you're done putting your list together, don't sit back—do
them. One by one—walk through your fears. Before you know
it, you'll discover that none of them has the power you thought.
We must constantly test our limits to see if they are real. I hope

you choose to exercise your courage and risk muscles! Going as far as you can go not only provides your life with momentum, but also builds character, helps you tap into your undiscovered abilities as well as your shortfalls, and helps you to recognize your likes/dislikes. There are a lot of exciting adventures out there just waiting for you—go out and find them!

**Be bold. If you're going to make an error,
make it a doozy, and don't be afraid to hit the ball.**
—*Billie Jean King*

**Even if you're on the right track,
you'll get run over if you just sit there.**
—*Will Rogers*

The best way to predict the future is to create it.
—*Unknown*

Let's just recognize that sometimes even the most desirable things can still be scary. Choosing a college…Deciding on a career…Getting married…Having a baby…These passages of life can all evoke fear in us, and they all carry with them an element of risk. However, we cannot let our fears hold us back from experiencing these joys. And let's face it, not all of us get it right the first time! But as a Hollywood film director once said, "If it doesn't work out the first time, you can always make a sequel." However, sometimes the element of risk seems even greater the second time around.

IF AT FIRST YOU DON'T SUCCEED, TRY TRY AGAIN

Remarriage clearly fits into this category. I know that, for me, the thought of finding a mate to last a lifetime seemed now even more daunting. But despite my skepticism, love found me. Boy, did it find·me! When I first looked up and saw Jeff Konigsberg, I said to my daughter Sarah, "Wow, why can't I meet a nice guy like that?" He seemed so confident and yet not cocky. His smile was so genuine it could light up Times Square. It was like one of those moments that was frozen in time. Even though it may sound silly, I think we both felt we were meant for each other from the moment our eyes met. Everything about him made me feel like life was great and we could conquer anything together.

It was, in my book, love at first sight—only to get better and better with time. And it did take Jeff some time to get comfortable with the whole idea of commitment, three and a half years to be exact (not that I was counting!). Ironically, Jeff would always say that it was easier for me to take "the leap," because I had been married before. And I guess in a way, that's right—because you've gone through the steps before. But quite frankly, I think that when you've experienced the pain of divorce, it seems even riskier to take those steps again. Being young and in love sometimes doesn't allow you to see beyond the moment. That's where the saying "love is blind" comes from—you are too blinded by love to see anything else.

When you enter marriage for the first time, you can't possibly understand the consequences of making the wrong decision. But once you've experienced the devastation and sadness of divorce, it seems like a much bigger risk the second time around because you feel much more vulnerable.

I think that many people getting married for the first time just assume that everything will always be wonderful. Whereas people who have been divorced (or are children of divorce) ask themselves, "How can I be sure that this one is for real? Will this one really last? Will he really love me forever? Will we grow together?" And of course for those single parents, there is always the question, "Will he love my children?"

Many of us refrain from ever asking these tough questions because we are afraid of grappling with the answers. But it's kind of like avoiding going to the doctor because you are afraid of hearing that something is wrong with you.

After my divorce, I thought that marriage was a childhood fantasy—that finding someone you could really count on and really grow with was just not possible. And when you feel like this, you build a gigantic wall around you. And it is very hard to let that wall down. But you can't experience the joys of love if you don't take that wall down. And taking it down is a *risk*.

Even if you "fall in love at first sight," taking down that wall can still be difficult. I found that I would feel safe, take it down—and then when I would feel his normal, male, first-time ambivalence, I would put it right back up. It took a while to discover that it was my ego that was the general contractor here! I'm so thankful that I learned to not only listen to my ego, but also to listen to my heart. My heart was telling me that Jeff was the one that I would truly grow with, feel safe with, respect…and therefore, it was *worth* the risk to work at taking that wall down for the final time.

Sometimes I feel people see me as stronger than I really am— immune to the insecurities and vulnerabilities that affect others. But in reality, I'm not any different. I hope that I can help you gain strength to take the necessary risks in your life by sharing my own struggles.

Life has two rules: number 1, Never quit!; number 2, Always remember rule number 1.
—*Duke Ellington*

~

TONY ROBBINS

Tony Robbins is a nationally known motivational author and speaker. With his bigger-than-life presence, he can command a room of 25,000 people to get up out of their chairs and present themselves to the stranger seated next to them like seasoned politicians. CEOs, top athletes, and even U.S. Presidents call upon Tony for motivation and inspiration. I asked him to share with you some of the methods he finds most helpful in fighting fear and taking risks.

~

Joan has already shared with you one of the questions that I tend to ask people when they're afraid: What would you do if you knew you couldn't fail? If you had no fear what would you do?

Fear itself keeps us from envisioning what is possible and prevents us from moving towards what we want. Whatever we focus on we feel.

There will be times in life when something will create not only fear for you, but will actually have a disastrous impact upon your life in the short term. The first thing amateur drivers learn in racing school—in order to be effective on the road—is how to come out of a spin.

As a driver, someone may crash in front of you, or there could be an oil slick on the track, and it may not be your fault; inevitably, however, it is going to affect both your path and your driving experience. So there will be a time in which you will go into a spin. The secret to coming out of a spin is to remember that when you go into spin, when you go into fear, when things start to turn in a direction you don't want, you must immediately focus on where you want to go instead of what you fear.

The tendency in life, of course, is to immediately focus on the wall that you don't want to hit. How many times have we read about people driving their sports car through the desert at 100 miles per hour and there is one telephone pole every quarter of a mile, yet they manage to hit that pole? The reason for this is because as soon as they start driving out of control, they focus on the pole that they want so desperately to avoid. Remember, whatever you focus on you steer into.

When I first had this experience, I said to myself, "no problem, I understand this," and I began to drive in a circle. The instructor beside me had four buttons, and if he pushed any one of those buttons, he could lift up one of the four wheels, causing us to spin out of control in that particular direction. He doesn't push the button when you're prepared, however; he waits until you're mentally fatigued.

Sure enough, he pushed the button, we started to spin out of control, and I immediately started to stare at the wall because I wanted to see myself die! Fortunately, he was in the car and he physically took his hand, pushing my jaw and head to the left where we needed to turn. I kept fighting him because, again, I wanted to see the comple-

tion of my life as we hit the wall! But, as he is pushing my face to the left, I automatically, unconsciously, steered to the left and in the final seconds the wheels caught, missing the wall by a few feet.

My instructor turned to me and asked, "did you learn?"

"Of course I did," I replied.

And, the next time out he pushed the button, I looked right at the wall again!

You have to train yourself to focus on what you want instead of what you fear. And the reason for this is to realize something very simple: If you focus on where you want to go, on what you want versus what you fear, are you guaranteed not to hit the wall? The answer, of course, is no. But, if you stare at the wall, you are guaranteed to crash into it.

The fastest way to deal with fear is turn the fear on itself. Start to identify that which you are afraid of with the following questions: If I don't do this, what will it cost me ultimately? What will it cost me in my relationships? What will it cost me with my kids? How unhappy will I be long term? What will happen to my self-esteem, my pride, my love? What will I miss out on, and what have I already missed out on because of this fear?

Answering such questions will help you see that the negative consequences of not acting far outweigh those of acting. We all do things to either avoid pain or gain pleasure, but our need to avoid pain is the greater of the two needs. When we're fearful, we're anticipating the worst possible consequence in order to avoid the pain we're imagining. But how often have you imagined a frightening situation only to experience it and realize, even if it was painful to go through, it was nowhere near as bad as your imagination created? Instead, unleash your imagination on the pain the fear will bring, the price it will cost you, and you will find a way to motivate yourself in spite of fear.

There are often times in life where we feel we have two choices. Either choice will be painful, but we always pick the one we believe will be least painful. But I tell you this: The most important difference in peoples' lives is a willingness to take risk. There is nothing in your life of significant value that you didn't risk to get. Whether it was walking across the room to a person you were interested in and expressing that interest, starting your own business, asking for the raise, or telling someone to stop doing something destructive in your life while knowing you could be rejected for speaking up. All these experiences provide risk—that is true—but they provide even greater reward.

When I encounter people who are afraid, I get them to focus on the reward instead of the risk. Here is a simple seven-step process that you can do to shift your focus:

STEP ONE: IDENTIFY WHAT YOU'RE AFRAID OF. Picture that fear in your mind, "freeze frame" it, and push it far away from you. You are literally taking what you're focusing on and changing the way you feel about it. Whatever the fear is, imagine that situation and push it away from you. The more distance you create between yourself and the fear, the less power that fear will *have. As you freeze frame it or shrink the fear in your mind, you will feel very differently.*

STEP TWO: CHANGE YOUR PHYSIOLOGY, THE WAY YOU USE YOUR BODY. *In order to be fearful you have to use your body in a very specific way, much like you would if you were in a depressed state.*

How do you use your body when you're really fearful? What do you do with your hands? Do you put them against your face, do you grip them tightly? Does your breathing become full or shallow? Do you tend to look down or up, do your shoulders collapse down or pull back?

When most people say, "I am feeling down or feeling stressed," notice they are contracting their body. But what you want to do, now that you have frozen the image and pushed it away, is stand tall. Stand as if you felt more confident than you have ever before in your life. Breathe deeply. Take a deep breath in and explode it out of your mouth with a sound like "shh." Shout a word like "yes" five times.

While this may seem overly simplistic, remember that the way we move determines the way we feel. If your facial expression is one of total determination, and you are breathing in a strong, full manner with your shoulders back and your head up, moving with a sense of absolute certainty, you will begin to experience this emotion. Thinking yourself into feeling better rarely works. But, putting your body there physically, will absolutely get you there.

STEP THREE: BREATHE! *Enhance your state by breathing, and imagine you're breathing from your heart. Scientific research has shown that when people are in a state of fear, their nervous systems become completely agitated. Breathing and focusing on the energy of your heart aligns the chaos in your nervous system* and centers you.

STEP FOUR: THINK OF A TIME WHEN YOU WERE SO AFRAID AND IT TURNED OUT NOT TO BE SO DIFFICULT. *Secondly, remember a time when you were afraid but you did it anyway and you experienced great rewards.*

By changing not only your body, but your focus, you'll start to feel very centered and very resourceful. In a resourceful state you can make better decisions.

If there is one thing I can tell you that makes a difference in life it is this: Decisions change our life. It is not our conditions, but our decisions, that shape the quality of our lives. And, it is in our moments of decision that our destiny is shaped.

When you are in fear, you make the wrong decision. A decision from fear is always the wrong decision, so get centered and get strong by remembering a time when you succeeded.

STEP FIVE: ASK YOURSELF: WHAT WOULD I GET BY DOING THIS? *Instead of thinking about the fear and the negative consequences, concentrate on what you will get if you push yourself through this fear. If you start your own business, for example, there will certainly be challenges, but ultimately what will you have? Total freedom. Time to be with your children. The pride of creating that which you envisioned.*

If you approach a person and express yourself, what will you get? At minimum, even if you don't connect with this person, you'll develop more muscle and more strength, and the ability to ask someone else. However, you may ultimately get the relationship you have always dreamed of. Just like the racecar driver, now that you're feeling strong, focus on what you want and where you are going instead of what you are afraid of.

STEP SIX: ASK YOURSELF: IF I WERE GOING TO TAKE ACTION IMMEDIATELY, A SMALL MOVE TOWARD THAT GOAL RIGHT NOW, WHAT ACTION WOULD I TAKE? *Would I get in the car? Would I call someone and have that person join me? Would I send an e-mail? Would I walk up right now and at least shake their hand and say hello? What first step would I take? Because if you take the first step, you will take the second, third, and fourth, and you'll gain momentum.*

STEP SEVEN: DO IT. *You feel good, you're strong, you have pushed the fear away, remembered times when you were successful, and you know what you're going to obtain by taking action. You also know what step to take—do it. You're in the state to do it. Do not give yourself an escape, do not give yourself a way out, and as soon as you take action, you'll start to build muscle.*

Each time you do this, each time you walk through these seven steps, you'll build momentum and this process will be automatic. You rule fear, fear does not rule you. And with that comes ultimate freedom and a life filled with passion. Now, that is not a life where there is no fear, it simply means you've learned how to handle the fear, driving that energy into something that pushes you forward instead of pulling you back.

There is little traffic on the extra mile.

—Unknown

Believe in Yourself and Others Will Too!

It's not what you are that holds you back,
it's what you think you are not.
—Denis Waitley

How do I love me? Let me count the ways. OK, so that's not how it really goes. But it's a good starting point for an examination of a person's self-esteem. Am I smart or stupid? Am I lovable? Am I worthy? Am I attractive? Am I a success or a failure? Don't most of us ask ourselves these questions at one time or another? Unlike our hearts and lungs, which self-regulate and function on their own, our minds do not automatically provide us with confident thinking and astute judgment, openness, willingness, or even worthiness. We've been left to our own resolve on this one. Well not completely...our parents get a good head start on it...and let's just all agree right now that most of us come from some sort of dysfunctional fam-

FACING PAGE: Horses sense their rider's fears—jumping trained me to project confidence to get over the next hurdle.

ily. But no matter what your handicap entering adulthood, psychologists agree that it is still possible to develop positive self-esteem.

The most important opinion you have is the
one you have of yourself, and
the most significant things you say all day
are those things you say to yourself.
—*Unknown*

Self-trust is the first secret of success.
—*Ralph Waldo Emerson*

What lies behind us and what lies before us are tiny
matters compared to what lies within us.
—*Anonymous*

The only limit to our realization of tomorrow
will be our doubts about today.
—*Franklin Delano Roosevelt*

Developing positive self-esteem is crucial since it plays a vital role in the important choices and decisions we make that shape our lives. It can empower and energize us or it can render us helpless. It's that force within that gives us the confidence to feel worthy and deserving of happiness, the resilience to cope with life's challenges, and the entitlement to assert our needs and enjoy our rewards. And when we fall down, it gives us the power to pick ourselves back up and the motivation to begin again.

We don't see things as they are, we see them as we are.
—Anais Nin

**The next time you get nervous about others' opinions,
look them mentally in the eye and say,
"What you think of me is none of my business."**
—Terry Cole Whitaker

Oh, I'm so inadequate and I love myself!
—*Meg Ryan*

Don't read anything the press writes about you
because nobody can be that bad
and nobody can be that good either.
—*Barbara Walters*

Don't be run so much by what you lack as by
what you have already achieved.
—*Marcus Aurelius*

We commonly think of self-esteem as "believing in ourselves." You'd think it would be easier to believe in yourself if you had already accomplished everything you wanted in life or were rich and famous. But we're told that's not the way it works. Belief in ourselves actually comes before accomplishment, not afterward.

Let me listen to me and not to them.
—*Gertrude Stein*

As for worrying about what other people might think—
forget it. They aren't concerned about you.
They're too busy worrying about what you and
other people think of them.
—*Michael LeBoeuf*

Never build a case against yourself.
—*Robert Rowbottom*

If you really do put a small value upon yourself,
rest assured that the world will not
raise your price.
—*Unknown*

Lack of confidence is not the result of difficulty;
the difficulty comes from a lack of confidence.
—*Seneca*

When our center is strong, everything else is secondary.
—*Elie Wiesel*

ELLEN MCGRATH, Ph.D.

Dr. Ellen McGrath was a contributing editor to "Good Morning America" for many years. I interviewed her on everything from couples counseling to building self-esteem in our teenage daughters to coping with crises. She is the author of *When Feeling Bad is Good*, *The Complete Idiot's Guide to Beating the Blues*, and *Women and Depression: Risk Factors and Treatment Issues*. She is also the president and founder of Bridge Coaching, a consulting firm for top business executives. Building self-esteem is the cornerstone of all of her counseling.

SELF-ESTEEM MUSCLE: USE IT OR LOSE IT!

The most important muscle you have is your self-esteem muscle but it's also one of the easiest ones to lose. There are countless reasons to feel bad about ourselves these days: we're told (or we decide) we're too fat/thin, too old/young, nerdy/turdy, weak/meek, overworked/useless.... Some days the list just seems endless! We also live in a hyper-competitive culture where our worth is measured too often by comparing status, possessions and, of course, the size of our bodies. This "I'm better than you are" approach can easily make us feel that we NEVER *have enough, whether it's time, money, promotions, happiness or relationships, and others always seem to have more.*

We also forget that maintaining self-esteem is a lifelong psychological workout, no matter who you are. Self-esteem is not an end goal. It's a mental muscle which must be developed and maintained through exercising it our whole lives. Self-esteem is an on-going process of learning to genuinely like and care for yourself, which must be renegotiated at each age and stage of life. When we build up the self-esteem muscle deep inside ourselves, we learn to like and respect who we are, no matter what is happening around us. We find that we must take good care of ourselves, because we value ourselves too much to even consider being neglectful or hurtful to our self.

So how can you learn to build and boost the self-esteem muscle? Here are four proven esteem boosters:

1. A PASSION A DAY KEEPS THE DOCTOR AWAY. *Even if it's just for 15 minutes, pursue one of your passions every day. Watch your health and esteem grow as you feed your soul through regular exercise of passionate interest. Whether it's a 15 minute "quickie" with your honey before work, reading a bedtime story to a loved child (even if it's over the phone), gardening after work, or reading your favorite author, focus on what activities mean the most to you and make them a daily priority.*

2. KEEP A REPORT CARD ON YOUR BEST EFFORTS. *Win, lose or draw, note the effort you are putting into an activity and give yourself credit when you try 100%. Each day, note your three*

best efforts and keep a report card of these efforts for one week. If you truly can't think of anything positive you have done, have someone you love do it for you and write it down each day. After studying the report card, you'll understand more about why they love you, which makes it a little easier to love yourself.

3. MAKE A SELF-ESTEEM BULLETIN BOARD. *Make a space to put esteem "in your face." This action strategy is especially helpful with insecure children/teens/adults or for the times we're depressed. The beauty of the bulletin board is that every day you have to look at why you should feel good about yourself: photos of those who love you, the cover page of a great report you wrote, a copy of your bonus check, your first walkathon t-shirt, a necklace from your first trip alone, a funny cartoon you doodled, a recipe you made that came out particularly well, your bowling or golf scores from an awesome game....Collect visible reminders of your worth, look at them everyday and soon self-esteem will feel more like a natural habit.*

4. *STOP* IN THE NAME OF LOVE! *Dispute negative thoughts about yourself with a red* STOP *sign every time a bad thought pops up. You can cut out a big* STOP *sign from red construction paper and tape it on your mirror or wall. Or make a small* STOP *sign from a post-it and keep it in your appointment book or on your desk or computer. Every time a negative thought about yourself appears, look at or imagine the sign and think* STOP, *even say "*STOP!*" Don't worry. With practice, you'll learn to mean it.*

Then exercise your self-esteem muscle and convert the negative thought to the exact opposite: a positive, affirming thought about yourself. Converting negative thinking to positive means "I'm too fat" becomes "I'm fine the way I am" and "I'm so stupid" switches to "So I made a mistake. I'll learn from it." The only way to learn to love yourself is to think and talk about yourself with the utmost respect and caring, whether you believe it or not. THINKING positive will eventually make you FEEL positive about yourself and your self-esteem muscle will become a priceless resource.

I couldn't wait for success so I went ahead without it.
—*Jonathan Winters*

**It is difficult to see things clearly if the
shadow of doubt diminishes the light entering your eyes.**
—*From The Key to Life*

No one can make you feel inferior without your consent.
—*Eleanor Roosevelt*

If we want to be open to relationships, opportunities, challenges, and risk-taking, we need to start with our own state of mind. That's our first risk because it is somewhat a leap of faith. But just remember, if we don't believe in ourselves, who will? Self-esteem is built on two foundations: (1) being open to reasonable risk and (2) taking the time to master the skills that risks require. Every time I have doubted whether I could accomplish something, my belief in myself has always been what has made it possible.

I'll never forget the time I met with William Crowell, deputy director of the National Security Agency in Washington, D.C. Only he could grant me access to the inner workings of the NSA building—so top secret that it didn't even have an official address—for one of my "Behind Closed Doors" specials. I had to put on much more than my most official navy blue suit. I had to put on my most confident demeanor. If he did not believe in my integrity and in my confidence to be able to portray fairly this most sensitive facility, I would never get inside those doors. By the time the meeting had ended, I had achieved my goal. Feeling comfortable with our mission, he took me "Behind Closed Doors" of the National Security Agency, into its most highly restricted areas. I was shown the enormous computer systems which are constantly decoding transmissions from every country around the world. The employees were so shocked to see a member of the press walking the halls that one of them, as he turned back for a double take, literally walked into a wall! (No, laughing would have been politically incorrect!)

**Confidence is the inner voice that says
you are becoming what you are capable of being.**
—*Unknown*

**If you do not believe in yourself,
do not blame others for lacking faith in you.**
—*Brendan Frances*

**The way you are is not the result of what has happened to
you, it's the result of what you decide to keep inside you.**
—*Unknown*

**It takes courage to grow up
and turn out who you really are.**
—*e.e. cummings*

If I had lacked that belief in myself, they would never have believed in me. William Shakespeare once said, "Our doubts are our traitors." Time and again, I have found that the most important attribute I need on a story is positive self-esteem—it's my best chance for success.

**In order to become the winner that you
will respect and admire...you must have control of
the authorship of your own destiny...the pen
that writes your life story
MUST be held in your own hand.**
—*Irene C. Kassorda*

How do successful people get there? One thing is for sure—they do not get there by accident. They start by deciding what it is they want, and by making choices that keep them on their path toward their goals.

It is up to you to decide what you want from life. Success is highly personal. It can be baking the perfect apple pie, successfully raising children, becoming the CEO of a bustling business or making an important scientific discovery. But no matter what your aspirations, I have come to believe that success is a state of mind, rather than a material pinnacle. Now, with that said, how about finding what you like to do best and getting someone to pay you to do it! Now we're talking!

Humanity is divided into three parts:
1. Those who make things happen,
2. Those who watch things happen, and
3. Those who don't know what's happening.
—*Unknown*

As I was growing up, like most children I would ask my mommy, "What can I be when I grow up?" She always responded the same way, "Anything you want to be—just hitch your wagon to a star." That is where it starts—discovering and finding our passions. A lot of people forget this basic first step! It is up to us to determine what we want out of life.

**If you don't run your own life,
someone else will.**
—*John Atkinson*

**Experience is not what happens to you;
it is what you do with what happens to you.**
—*Aldous Huxley*

**The only place success
comes before work is in the dictionary.**
—*Satchell Paige*

I've always been a big fan of the late author, Dr. David Viscott, who wrote the book *Emotional Resilience*. In it he said that our purpose in life is to find our gift, perfect it, and give it back to others. Those words have helped me define what I want to do with my life. At one time, it was to be a successful television broadcaster and hold a top position and get paid top dollar. Later, I revised this goal to be a communicator who inspires others and can make a difference in the lives of others. I'm continually searching and finding new ways to achieve this goal.

It is never too late
to be what you might have become.
—*George Eliot*

Many of life's failures are people who
did not realize how close
they were to success when they gave up.
—*Thomas Edison*

For every person who climbs the ladder of success,
there are a dozen waiting for the elevator.
—*Unknown*

I always wanted to be somebody,
but I should have been more specific.
—*Lily Tomlin*

This process takes more than just saying, "I want to be some-body." We need to define what we each have to offer and what we feel passionate about. Once we decide, we need to *believe* that it is possible and begin working toward that end. I once heard the only place success comes before work is in the dictio-nary. We can't wait for good things to happen, we can't wait until we get lucky—we need to work toward our goal and make our own luck.

Making a success of something has
nothing to do with luck. Care, thought, and study
go into making something succeed;
luck is something you get
playing the lottery or roulette.
—*Unknown*

Opportunities are usually disguised as hard work,
so most people don't recognize them.
—*Ann Landers*

If you can't do great things,
do small things in a great way.
Don't wait for great opportunities.
Seize common, everyday ones and make them great.
—*Napolean Hill*

When I was about 10 years old, I had a friend over to my house to play one Saturday afternoon. When she walked in the door, she looked around and said, "Boy, you have a really nice house—you guys are really lucky." Later that evening, my dad took me aside and said, "You should tell your friend that the harder I work, the luckier we get." I'll never forget that. I'm thankful that success was something my parents taught me to plan for and work hard to achieve.

My grandfather once told me that there are
two kinds of people: those who do the work
and those who take the credit.
He told me to try to be in the first group;
there was much less competition there.
—Indira Gandhi

If we did all we were capable of doing,
we would literally astonish ourselves.
—*Thomas Edison*

There are no secrets to success.
It is the result of preparation, hard work,
and learning from failure.
—*Colin L. Powell*

PLAN FOR SUCCESS

A *plan* is, in fact, what comes next. No one starts a new business or even expands one without a business plan. And one thing I've learned is that if we don't have a plan for ourselves, we will probably be part of someone else's.

My father (actor Danny Thomas) told me,
"I raised you to be a thoroughbred.
Thoroughbreds wear blinders: they don't
look at the other horses. They run their own races."
I've tried to run my own race my whole life.
—*Marlo Thomas*

I've always tried to go a step past
wherever people expected me to end up.
—*Beverly Sills*

I'm not going to limit myself, just because
people won't accept the fact that I can do something else.
—*Dolly Parton*

With your desires and talents identified, with a plan in mind, and a belief that you can achieve your goal, then there is one thing left—*doing it*. The ladder of success doesn't care who climbs it—so get going! Opportunities come along whether you're ready for them or not. They are seldom labeled. Whether they happen to you, or you make them happen, that old saying, "luck is when preparation meets opportunity," happens to be true. To seize success, you must be ready when *your* opportunity comes along.

Swing hard, in case they throw the ball
where you're swinging.
—*Duke Snider*

Hit the ball over the fence and
you can take your time going around the bases.
—*John W. Roper*

To be no one but yourself in a world
which is doing its best to make
you just like everybody else, means to
fight the greatest battle there is or ever will be.
—*e e. cummings*

These days, with the world moving at such a fast pace, and competition so fierce, *a person who says something can't be done, will probably be interrupted by someone doing it.* I know I've had ideas that I thought were great but too difficult—only to later see that someone else accomplished them. What held me back? I was probably afraid of making a mistake or, worse, that I would fail.

The difference between the impossible and the
possible lies in a person's determination.
—*Tommy Lasorda*

The only failure which lacks dignity is the failure to try.
—*Unknown*

If opportunity doesn't knock...build a door.
—*Milton Berle*

Determination to stick to my goals, an openness to new ways to achieve them, a willingness to make mistakes along the way, and an acceptance of constructive criticism have all helped me find my way. And, of course, a little inspiration along the way is always helpful. I think we can all be motivated by other people's thoughts on the power of following their dreams. And it's just plain common sense that we are able to learn from other people's failures and achievements.

**If you wish success in life,
make PERSEVERANCE your bosom friend,
EXPERIENCE your wise counselor,
CAUTION your elder brother, and
HOPE your guardian genius.**
—*Joseph Addison*

Things do not happen. Things are made to happen.
—*John F. Kennedy*

God gives all birds their food, but he does not drop it into their nests.
—*Unknown*

ZIG ZIGLAR

A world-class motivational speaker, Zig Ziglar travels around the world, delivering his message of hope, humor, and enthusiasm. Hundreds of corporations worldwide use his books, videos, and audiotapes to train their employees to be more successful. He is a genius at persuading people to making a commitment to be the best they can be. A few years ago, I was asked to speak at a motivational seminar; I was daunted when I realized I would be following Zig Ziglar, the master motivator. Intimidating? Oh yeah. But his presence helped put me "over the top" that day! Now I'd like to share with you an excerpt from his best-seller *Over The Top*. This checklist will help guide you in living a happy and successful life.

THE TOP

You are at the top when...

1. You clearly understand that failure is an event, not a person; that yesterday ended last night, and today is your brand-new day.

2. You have made friends with your past, are focused on the present, and optimistic about your future.

3. You know that success (a win) doesn't make you, and failure (a loss) doesn't break you.

4. You are filled with faith, hope, and love; and live without anger, greed, guilt, envy, or thoughts of revenge.

5. You are mature enough to delay gratification and shift your focus from your rights to your responsibilities.

6. You have made friends of your adversaries, and have gained the love and respect of those who know you best.

7. You understand that others can give you pleasure, but genuine happiness comes when you do things for others.

8. You are pleasant to the grouch, courteous to the rude, and generous to the needy.

9. You love the unlovable, give hope to the hopeless, friendship to the friendless, and encouragement to the discouraged.

10. You can look back in forgiveness, forward in hope, down in compassion, and up with gratitude.

Change Is Inevitable, Suffering Is Optional

Blessed are the flexible,
for they shall not be bent out of shape.
—Unknown

Whenever I'm speaking to a group of people about change, I always begin with, "Have you ever noticed the only person who likes change is a wet baby?" And it always gets a laugh. Why? I think it's because everyone recognizes that although change is the one thing constant in our lives—it usually produces a tremendous amount of fear and discomfort.

**Our own dilemma is that we hate change
and love it at the same time; what we really want is for
things to remain the same but get better.**
—*Sidney J. Harris*

When we are no longer able to change a situation, we are
challenged to change ourselves.
—*Victor Frankl*

People don't change because they see the light.
They change because they feel the heat.
—*Unknown*

It can be something as simple as cutting your hair, or moving to
a new city, starting a new job, marrying, divorcing, or losing a
loved one. It always seems unnerving when we're dealing with
life's inevitable upheavals. You might think that someone like
me, who is willing to leap off tall mountains and bungee bridges,
would look at life's changes as new and exciting! Yeah, right—
I'm as reluctant as the next guy to accept change, but I have
learned that change always seems more difficult at the outset.
But if I work hard at remaining positive and if I view changes as
opportunities to learn, grow, and reformulate my life, I've found
that I've had a much easier time dealing with them.

If you can't change your fate, change your attitude.
—*Amy Tan*

Life is change. Growth is optional. Choose wisely.
—*Karen Kaiser Clark*

A bend in the road is not the end of the road,
as long as you make the turn.
—*Unknown*

Albert Einstein said, "In the middle of every difficulty lies an opportunity," although sometimes it doesn't feel like that when you're drowning in the fear of the unknown. But I actually think he's right. Out of every seeming crisis comes the choice to reconceive ourselves as individuals. I've learned never to underestimate our power to change ourselves.

Life's challenges are not supposed to paralyze you.
They're supposed to help you discover who you are.
—*Bernice Johnson Reagan*

Not everything that is faced can be changed,
but nothing can be changed until it is faced.
—*James Baldwin*

When one door closes, another opens;
but we often look so long and so regretfully
upon the closed door that
we do not see the ones which open for us.
—*Alexander Graham Bell*

I wish they would have taught us the ABC's we really needed to know. **A**ccept that change is inevitable. **B**elieve that you can create miraculous change in your life. **C**ommit to being flexible. Once you begin learning how to cope with change, you can begin to welcome it into your life, seek the unknown, and experiment with life.

In life, we cannot avoid loss.
Freedom and happiness are found in the flexibility
and ease with which we move through change.
—*From A Hero In Every Heart*

Unless you're the lead dog,
your view never changes.
—*Unknown*

**Tough times are like speed bumps...
They only slow you down a little...
They don't throw you off course.**
—*Unknown*

I once read that "the beauty of life is its changes" and that "the art of life lies in a constant readjustment to our surroundings." Nice thoughts. In fact, life *is* beautiful and profound. Of course, I would be less than truthful if I said I thought the readjustment part was always easy. But we're all a part of this ever-changing journey, and our emotional resilience depends upon our ability to accept what happens to us along the way—and to emotionally renegotiate our reality.

**You may have a fresh start at any moment you choose,
for this thing that we call "failure" is not the falling down,
but the staying down.**
—*Mary Pickford*

Arrange whatever pieces come your way.
—*Virginia Woolf*

To each of us, at certain points of our lives,
there come opportunities to rearrange our formulas
and assumptions—not necessarily to be rid of the old, but
more to profit from adding something new.

—*Leo Buscaglia*

One of the best ways to not let life catch you off guard is to expect change and, if possible, anticipate and plan for it. Also effective is taking a look back at the change that's already occurred in your life and how you've dealt with it. This allows us to better understand which formulas worked and which ones got us in trouble. Here's a glimpse of my ever-changing path—and, yes, I certainly learned from this exercise.

EVERYDAY IS A WINDING ROAD

LEAVING THE NEST: As I approached my high school graduation, my mom found an opportunity where I could study and travel around the world, aboard a ship. Students spent four months on this World Campus Afloat, and she felt it would broaden my horizons. Having skipped a few grades, I was only 16 and would be the youngest aboard. Scary thought? You bet—but what an opportunity! The experience changed the course of my life.

ENTERING THE WORLD: After a few brief stints—in an x-ray lab, a stock brokerage firm, and a department store—I heard that the local TV station was under pressure to put women on the news. With no idea what was in store for me, I managed to get an interview with the news director. I think he was a bit flabbergasted when I asked him what the industry had to offer me! My straightforward approach and my experience travelling the world paid off and I got my first job in television. Little did I know where this would take me.

THE BIG APPLE CALLS: From weather girl to consumer reporter to news anchor, I was just beginning to feel confident and

comfortable...when the next opportunity knocked. The ABC affiliate in New York City offered me a position as a reporter. In one phone call, I would go from *big* fish in little pond to *tiny* little fish in gigantic pond! As unfamiliar as I was with the Big Apple, I was even more unfamiliar with street reporting. Would I like it? Would I be good at it? But if I didn't take it, would this kind of opportunity ever knock again?

ONWARD AND UPWARD: After a rough first year on the streets of New York, learning to report on and deal with the crises and the crazies, I was finally beginning to catch on. But, just as I was beginning to feel at home, executives at the ABC network offered me a role on "Good Morning America." Interviewing heads of state...live? Now that's scary! It was a chance of a lifetime but also a bit chancy—what if I failed? Would I be wagering my whole career on my ability to pull this one off? That's a pretty big wager.

IT'S A GIRL!: As if the spotlight wasn't bright enough, the job offer was immediately followed by a phone call that I was expecting! I'm gonna be a mommy! I'm gonna be a host of "Good

Morning America"! I'm gonna be a *big* mommy on national television? That much I knew…but I never could have imagined the media attention my pregnancy would have received. When my daughter Jamie was born and ABC wanted me back on the air ASAP, I saw no alternative but to bring her with me. To me, I was just putting one foot in front of the other, trying to cope with my ever-changing life, and yet, to some, I changed the way business viewed and dealt with working moms.

JOINING THE BIG LEAGUES: When David Hartman stepped down, I had to step up to the plate. It reminded me of something I once heard, "Not getting what you desire and getting what you desire can both be disconcerting." Would I hold the audience through this transition? When Charlie Gibson became my new team-mate, my role on the show changed dramatically. Now officially an equal host, I had far greater responsi-bilities and more important stories. This, of course, required more self-confidence and more sleep—okay, one out of two ain't bad!

THINGS FALL APART: After having been such a public mom for 10 years, it wasn't easy to announce that my marriage was ending. The press had put me on a pedestal, juggling career and motherhood with seeming aplomb. I knew that my divorce was going to be perceived as a fall from grace, but I could never have prepared myself for the avalanche of the hurtful, harmful, and intrusive public coverage of my personal sorrow. It saddened me to become so disillusioned by my fellow man, sensing their apparent enjoyment in my ongoing melodrama. But then, again, it forced me to be stronger. Out of our adversity we find our strength.

GETTING BACK ON THE DANCE FLOOR: You'd think I would've known by now...but I was blindsided by the public curiosity of my new life as a single woman. And how is anyone supposed to find a lifetime mate in this glass fishbowl? But obviously I had to move on. However, picking up dating in your 40s, when you left off in your 20s, makes you feel as vulnerable as a teenager.

TIME TO SAY GOODBYE: Leaving "Good Morning America" after almost 20 years and 4000 broadcasts would represent one of the biggest changes I would ever make. I knew by now that how I handled this change would be anything but private. However, this time the outpouring of support from my viewers gave me much strength and confidence to tackle the obvious question. What will I do with the rest of my life?

LET'S TRY SOMETHING NEW: While everyone waited to see what show I would move to, I would instead embark on a new way to live—only choosing projects that challenged me and afforded me a quality of life. Interestingly, because people didn't see me "on the job," they would ask, "Are you enjoying retirement?" I've learned to smile. I like my new path.

WALKING DOWN THE AISLE AGAIN: I think among the public circus that my life had become, I had lost hope of finding a true love who would stand by me through the good and bad. But just when you least expect it, life pulls through. I found Jeff— in a deli no less! Our love and commitment to each other holds strong, and, interestingly, being able to trust in him has helped me to regain trust in other people.

LOVIN' CHANGE!: New business ventures, new challenges, new chapters in my life. But the biggest change is that I'm not daunted by these changes, but rather excited by them...that's the best change of all.

> **To exist is to change, to change is to mature,**
> **to mature is to go on creating oneself endlessly.**
> —*Henri Bergson*

> **One has to remember that every failure can be a**
> **stepping stone to something better.**
> —*Colonel Harland Sanders*

> **Few journeys through life are uninterrupted.**
> **Take these pauses as a time to reflect, refresh, and recharge—**
> **and they cease to be perceived as interruptions.**
> —*From* The Key to Life

> **Out of every crisis comes the choice to be reborn,**
> **to reconceive ourselves as individuals,**
> **to choose the kind of change that will help us to**
> **grow and fulfill ourselves more completely.**
> —*Nena O'Neill*

You must want to fly so much that
you are willing to give up being a caterpillar.
—*Trina Paulus*, From Hope For The Flowers

DEALING WITH STRESS

I'm an old man who has known a great many problems,
most of which never happened.
—*Mark Twain*

If you think you're the only one who's feeling stressed out, relax and just know that stress affects everyone. No one is immune from it. Stress is inevitable, but you don't have to be a victim of it. We can learn to identify and deal with our stresses so that we don't end up like Mark Twain.

That the birds fly overhead, this you cannot stop.
That they build a nest in your hair, this you can prevent.
—*Chinese proverb*

If you ask a dozen people to list the causes of stress, you'll probably get a dozen different answers: frustration, fear, panic, anxiety, anger, revenge, impatience, feelings of being overwhelmed, powerlessness, sadness, lack of control, or even boredom. They might also cite having difficulty dealing with any kind of change in their lives. And of course, there's the good old basic fear of the unknown: being taken out of your routine and disconnected from what makes you feel most comfortable. Unfortunately, it's staying in your routine that keeps you from growing and moving forward in your lives.

**Life is about not knowing, having to change,
taking the moment and making the best of it, without
knowing what's going to happen next.**
—*Gilda Radner*

Worry often gives a small thing a big shadow.
—*Swedish proverb*

My tormentor is myself left over from yesterday.
—*Deepak Chopra*

So, what's stressing you out? Come on...Is it making decisions...asserting yourself...being alone...intimacy?

I'll go first; okay, that seems only fair. Here's a glimpse into the kinds of things that stress me out:

1. Am I making the right decisions with my teenage girls? Do I have the stamina to say "no" to them and stick to it?

2. Am I handling finances wisely? Am I planning for my future properly?

3. Is my upcoming speech as good as it can be?

4. Now that I've taken on the role of president of Women's Supermarket Network, am I living up to this new responsibility?

5. Will I finish this book on time?

6. I hate my latest haircut; how long will it take to grow out?

Frazzle-Free Mornings....

FOUR SIMPLE STEPS TO SHORT-CIRCUIT YOUR DAILY STRESSES.

○ Plan your work and work your plan—I always find I'm not so overwhelmed in the morning if I plan my day the night before. I'm notorious for my to do list, but it keeps me focused and organized as opposed to frazzled and harried.

○ Lay out your clothes the night before—I developed this habit while hosting "Good Morning America." Of course, back then, I literally laid them on the bathroom floor in the order in which they would go on my body. Even the smallest decision is tough at 3:45 a.m.! For you, it may mean organizing your briefcase or your exercise bag for the following day.

○ Go to bed!—Sleep deprivation takes a heavy toll on us. Sleep experts say that your inner clock should be able to awaken you in the morning, as opposed to your alarm clock. I solved this problem by smashing my alarm clock on "The Late Show with David Letterman" when I left "Good Morning America."

○ Eat breakfast—After fasting all night, your body needs fuel to start the day. Fuelling your body revs your metabolism and increases your energy level and your ability to focus and think.

Once we put our finger on what stresses us, then we need to understand what it does to our bodies. Psychologists will tell you that the stress response in the human body is something called "fight or flight." It's that physical response to anything that threatens us. The heart begins to pump faster, your blood pressure rises, your breathing quickens and your muscles tighten...and that's just the beginning. We've all been there— we've all felt it. But we haven't all learned to deal with it, and chronic stress spells *trouble*. It's been said that over 75 percent of all chronic disease is stress related. So if you find that you're constantly sick, don't forget to take a long, hard look at the stress in your life. Scientists are learning more and more everyday about the mind/body connection—how our thoughts and emotions can dramatically affect our physical health.

A day of worry is more exhausting than a week of work.
—*Unknown*

Walk away from it until you are stronger.
All your problems will be there when you get back,
but you'll be better able to cope.
—*Lady Bird Johnson*

Most of the shadows of this life are
caused by our standing in our own sunshine.
—*Unknown*

✳ ✳ ✳ ✳ ✳ ✳

If you expect to be upset,
you'll seldom disappoint yourself..
—*Unknown*

So what are the tools that we can use to calm our nerves and open our minds? Here comes the good news...we all have the inner resources that are needed: courage, optimism, humility, humor, intuition, acceptance, forgiveness, love, and, yes, patience. These inner resources are to our souls what medicine is to our bodies.

We need to call upon these muscles if we want them to be strong. The more I strengthen mine, the more I can count on them in my next challenging moment—probably sometime later today. When my children roll their eyes and treat me like a moron, I look to my patience and my acceptance that teenagers need to feel like they don't need their mommies any longer to make decisions. I try to put the behavior in context, and then not to stoop to childlike behavior myself—like, ya know, getting in the last word! I mean, what up with that?!

Conflict cannot survive,
without your participation.
—*Unknown*

Life teaches us to be less harsh with
ourselves and with others.
—*Lin Yutang*

When you get to the end of your rope,
tie a knot and hang on!
—*Franklin D. Roosevelt*

So if your boss doesn't seem to be noticing all your hard work (not that he or she doesn't have anything else to worry about), or your mate isn't guessing whatever is bugging you (because of course we all expect our mates to have ESP—they should know us well enough to know what we're thinking, right?), then go to your inner muscles. Remember that it's not what is happening in these circumstances that is causing you stress but your *reaction* to what's happening. Are your expectations of life unrealistic? Should you really be expecting your busy boss to remember to stop and give thanks to your work well done? Should you really be expecting your mate to automatically see in your eyes what stressed you during your day?

**Everything that irritates us about others
can lead us to an understanding of ourselves.**
—*Carl Jung*

And then there are the emotions we carry around all the time that cause us stress: anger, resentment, and jealousy. Try to remember when your girlfriend shows you her new diamond bracelet that her loving husband gave her for Valentine's Day that she's wanting to share her joy with you, not necessarily rubbing your nose in the fact that your mate didn't do the same for you. (He did, however, pick his dirty socks up off the floor to show you he still cared.) You never know, your friend may have had a huge fight with her mate and the diamond bracelet could have been a peace offering. I know it's more difficult to think introspectively when you're in the middle of stress-producing circumstances, but it can save you from problems that never happened.

Worry is the misuse of your imagination.
—*Unknown*

The way I see it, if you want the rainbow,
you gotta put up with the rain.
—Dolly Parton

What you can't get out of, get into wholeheartedly.
—Unknown

Understanding that we, ourselves, bring on the stress, and that all too often the circumstances didn't warrant it, is heartening. With this knowledge, we can be empowered; we can short circuit the stress reaction and save ourselves from the headache we would otherwise have had.

So the next time you feel like strangling the living **** out of someone, remember that you're the one who actually suffers. Emotional maturity is accepting our feelings and then letting them go so that we can focus on the next moment with openness and receptivity.

When you don't have red, use blue.
—Unknown

If I had a formula for bypassing trouble,
I would not pass it 'round.
Trouble creates a capacity to handle it.
—*Oliver Wendell Holmes*

I have always grown from my problems
and challenges, from the things that
don't work out—that's when I've really learned.
—*Carol Burnett*

What the caterpillar calls the end of the world,
the master calls a butterfly.
—*Richard Bach*

BRIAN LUKE SEAWARD, Ph.D

Every now and then you come across an author whose words transform your life and inspire you forever. For me, that book was *Stand Like Mountain, Flow Like Water: Reflections on Stress and Human Spirituality* by Brian Luke Seaward, Ph.D. Dr. Seaward is also a faculty member of the University of Colorado—Boulder. In speeches across the country, I have referred to his teachings. Interestingly, many of those people who subsequently purchased his books later contacted Mr. Seaward to express their gratitude. Finally, he could take it no more and called me in my New York office to say "thank you" for my kind words. Believe it or not, this was a man who didn't own a television, so while my name sounded familiar, he had no idea that I was a television host! Much to my delight, he then asked me to write the forward to his upcoming book, *Stressed Is Desserts Spelled Backwards*. This was a most self-fulfilling honor and ironically, a most stressful task. I must have rewritten it 50 times!

Teachers like Brian Luke Seaward – who touch our hearts and change so many lives, are the unsung heroes of humanity. He's passionate, witty, humorous, and perhaps, most of all, inspiring. He looks like James Taylor, dresses like Indiana Jones, and writes like Mark Twain. In the role of traveler, visionary, mystic, and healer, Dr. Seaward has created a legacy in the field of wellness. Below he shares his thoughts on dealing with stress.

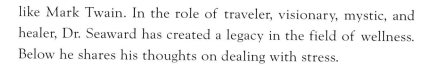

RAINBOWS AND STARS
Brian Luke Seaward, Ph.D

In my office I have a large poster of the Milkyway Galaxy. Toward the end of one of the spirals of stars and planets is a tiny yellow arrow, with a small sign which reads: You are here. *The poster is both a subtle and dynamic reminder to keep things in perspective. A student named Susan gave me this poster several years ago. As a college professor who teaches a course in stress management, perspective is one of the hallmark themes of the course.*

To describe Susan as a worry-wart was no exaggeration. In her mind, simple everyday issues became neurotic obsessions. To other people, small problems are typically viewed as molehills, yet to Susan, every concern became one more mountain to traverse in the Himalayan range. From rush hour traffic and the lack of available parking spaces to unanswered voice mail messages and missed breakfasts, her petty fears obscured her view of the bigger picture of life, specifically the joys and smiles that also constitute the balance of life's journey.

One day while shopping in downtown Chicago, Susan met a high school friend, now in a wheelchair crippled with Multiple Sclerosis. The ensuing conversation felt like a wet towel across Susan's face—a shocking revelation that quickly brought perspective to her own life. All of a sudden the problems she carried with her faded away. In their place she began to store thoughts of gratitude, compassion and faith. Later that day, she came across the poster of the Milkyway Galaxy. She bought two. The other is framed and hangs in her office. Some of life's best lessons may be introduced in the classroom, but the real learning occurs in everyday life situations.

There is an old proverb which states, "Be humble, for you are made of earth. Be noble for you are made of stars." The proverb speaks of balance—an inherent part of human nature. Balance is also a theme I teach in my stress management class. Although we all know the importance of balance, it's essence can quickly dissipate in the course of a hectic day. In an age of information overload, perhaps one of the most important aspects of life to seek balance is mental clarity, which in turn provides perspective on life's journey.

Over the years I have come across many themes for meditation and reflection, all of which lend balance to mind, body and spirit. My favorite is called the Rainbow Visualization. It only takes a few minutes to do, and with practice provides calm and stability during the winds of change.

The rainbow meditation involves seven comfortably slow deep breaths, seven affirmations and your imagination to visualize yourself *surrounded by seven colors of the rainbow. First, find a quiet place to sit or lay down and focus on your breathing.*

1. Focus your attention at the base of your spine. Then imagine yourself surrounded in a beautiful deep rich red light. Take a slow deep breath, and as you exhale, think the phrase, "I am grounded." Like roots from a tree deep in the earth, feel a sense of support and stability throughout your mind, body and spirit.

2. Next, direct your attention at the midpoint (center) of your body. Imagine yourself in a bright lush orange light. Take a slow deep breath, and as you exhale, think the phrase, "I am centered," feeling a sense of empowerment emanating throughout your body as you say this phrase.

3. Next, place your attention on your upper stomach. Then, imagine yourself surrounded in a brilliant yellow-golden light. Take a slow deep breath, and as you exhale, think the phrase, "I am loved." As you say this, feel a sense of acceptance and nurturance from friends and family.

4. Now, focus your attention on your heart space. Then, imagine yourself bathed in a lush emerald green light. Take a slow deep breath, and as you exhale, think the phrase, "I choose to love." With this thought, send a message of love, compassion or humor from your heart space to a friend.

5. Next, place your attention on your throat area. Then, imagine yourself surrounded in a warm light the color of aqua-blue. Take a

slow deep breath, and as you exhale, think the phrase, "My life has a meaningful purpose." As you repeat this, feel your worthiness to humanity.

6. *Now, direct your attention to your forehead. Then, imagine yourself surrounded in a pristine indigo blue hue. Take a slow deep breath, and as you exhale, think the phrase, "I am balanced." And feel a sense of balance is all that you do.*

7. *Finally, hold your attention at the very top of your head. Then, imagine yourself enveloped in the most beautiful violet light. Take a slow deep breath, and as you exhale, think the phrase, "I am connected," knowing that you are never alone.*

Let It Go Already!

**The mind is slow in unlearning
what it has been long in learning.**
—Seneca

We've all heard the expression, "Can't get out of your own way." Have you given much thought to what it really means? What do you think is in the way of your finding happiness or success? Perhaps some sadness that you're holding onto and reliving…or is it anger that seems to be raging inside you…and you just can't find it in yourself to forgive and forget? Holding a grudge and harboring resentment are two of the most common emotions people have trouble releasing. We tend to get angry when we're stressed out and exhausted. With this short fuse, we find ourselves snapping or yelling at those we love the most. Then, of course, we feel guilt and get angry at ourselves.

FACING PAGE: Taking the plunge can feel great.

You will soon break the bow if you keep it always stretched.
—*Phaedrus*

Holding resentment is like eating poison
and then waiting for the other person to keel over.
—*Unknown*

A heart filled with anger has no room for love.
—*Unknown*

To forgive but not to forget is like
burying the hatchet with the handle sticking out.
—*Unknown*

Do you harbor guilt feelings that are perhaps eating away at you? Might you have insecurities that you've blown up into proportions that are unreasonable, yet effective in keeping you where you are? And then, of course, there are all of the expectations about how life should have been. Are you trying to also meet

everyone else's expectations? Do you constantly look outside yourself for validation, and then in trying to be what others think you should be, lose yourself in the process?

As all of these negative thoughts race through your mind, did you ever stop to think that these forces that seem to drag you down are usually your own creations? Well, listen. You need to *stop*. Nobody ever said life was fair—or orderly, or perfect. Life is under no obligation to give us what we expect. However, life hardly ever lives up to our anxieties.

**I have a new philosophy.
I'm only going to dread one day at a time.**
—*Charlie Brown (Charles Schulz)*

**Look at life through the windshield
not the rear view mirror.**
—*Unknown*

**You cannot take charge of the present if
you are busy reliving the setbacks of the past.**
—*Newman & Berkowitz*

Wanna fly,
you got to give up the shit that weighs you down.
—*Toni Morrison*

The barriers you erect in order to protect yourself sometimes become very costly. One of my favorite authors, Jonathan Kabat-Zinn wrote about this in a book called *Wherever You Go, There You Are*. The title suggests that wherever you go, you take yourself and all of your emotions with you. So if you have certain fears, expectations, or destructive mental habits, all these tendencies will follow you and color how you see and react to the world. Holding onto anger, resentment, and hurt gives you tense muscles, a headache, and a sore jaw from clenching your teeth. It literally wears down your immune system and leaves you physically vulnerable.

I can certainly attest to this. I remember that when I was dealing with the upheaval of my divorce, I experienced painful muscle spasms in my neck and back. I turned to a chiropractor who told me he felt that, while he could ease my pain, I needed to treat the real cause—clenching my jaw. Upon entering my dentist's office, he took one look at my smile and exclaimed, "Boy, do you grind your teeth!" He fit me for a bite plate to prevent the clenching, and within days the spasms subsided. It wasn't until a few years later, and numerous self-help books later, that I learned I could let go of the stressful emotions all by myself—no bite plate needed.

Don't choose to be right, choose to be happy.
—*Unknown*

He is happy whose circumstances suit his temper;
but he is more excellent who
can suit his temper to any circumstances.
—**David Hume**

Conversely, if you are generally a realistic, positive person as you move through life, you'll probably be comfortable with the people and circumstances you encounter. You'll be flexible and open to life and whatever it decides to bring to you. Have the ability to let go and find forgiveness—you'll take back laughter and lightness into your daily life.

Dwell on the positive...you gain power.

Cling to the negative, all you'll have is a headache.

Our greatest problems in life come not so much
from the situations we confront
as from our doubts about our ability to handle them.
—Susan Taylor

You see what you believe,
rather than believe what you see.
—Dr. Wayne Dwyer

I've been told that we have over 50,000 thoughts each day. Obviously, if we're thinking mostly negative thoughts as we move through life, it is only natural that it will affect how we experience life. Whenever we cling too tightly to negative emotions, we become unsatisfied and uptight—and then, so do those around us. There are some people who have made a life out of negativity—they're called existentialists! I remember reading Jean-Paul Sartre in college. Not too long ago I ran across this excerpt about Sartre which really made me laugh: "Upon arriving in heaven, Jean-Paul Sartre commented, 'It's not what I expected!' God replied, 'Well what did you expect?' Sartre: 'Nothing.'" If you didn't find that funny, than perhaps you too are a victim of negative thinking.

**It's hard to defeat an enemy
who has an outpost in your own head.**
—*Sally Compton*

**Tension is who you think you should be.
Relaxation is who you are.**
—*Ancient Chinese proverb*

**Men are disturbed not by the things that happen,
but by their opinions of the things that happen.**
—*Epictetus*

So how do you open your mind and your heart to that which life presents? Mark Twain said, "Drag your thoughts away from your troubles—by the ears, by the heels or any other way you can manage it. It's the healthiest thing a body can do." Dwelling on the negative only contributes to its power. Thus, the phrase, "making a mountain out of a mole hill." When you let go of unrealistic expectations and negative emotions, you gain your power back. Former UCLA basketball coach John Wooden, who was known for his motivational tactics with his team, once said, "Things turn out best for the people who make the best of the way things turn out."

The greatest discovery of my generation is that human beings can alter their lives by altering their attitudes.
—*William James*

Of course, first you need to ask, "does your attitude need altering?" Before you can break out of prison, you must realize you're locked up.

If you want to be strong, know your weaknesses.
—*Unknown*

Experience is the name
everyone gives to their mistakes.
—*Oscar Wilde*

Even loss and betrayal can bring us awakening.
—*Buddha*

Oh for a life of sensations,
rather than of thoughts.
—*John Keats*

A bad habit never disappears miraculously.
It's an undo-it-yourself project.
—*Abigail Van Buren*

Many people are unaware of the emotions that hold them prisoner. In your quiet moments, examine your thoughts. No one is creating this anger or stress within you. Only you can do that.

Are you unwilling to let go of some unresolved past feelings which are constantly intruding on your present thoughts? Are you having trouble accepting and embracing what life has to offer you because it's not what you expected? Expectations are real killers—they are setups for disappointment. Anything you think you "must have" usually comes to own you. This kind of thinking renders you unable to see other happiness that comes your way—it leaves you dissatisfied with anything other than what you thought should have been.

**Life consists not in holding good cards;
but in playing those you hold...well.**
—*Josh Billings*

**We must give up last night
in order for us to be ready for tonight.**
—Unknown

It's never too late to give up our prejudices.
—*Henry David Thoreau*

**Fear is the dark room
where negatives are developed.**

—*Unknown*

**My barn having burned to the ground,
I can see the moon.**

—*Chinese proverb*

I want to share with you an exercise that I participated in during a taping for "Behind Closed Doors." The segment was on the complexities of addiction, and the episode was filmed at the Betty Ford Center. One of the techniques used with the patients involved writing letters to family members and friends about the unresolved feelings they carried with them. With this exercise they began to understand the emotions that were driving them to their addiction. When nightfall came, the participants joined hands around a roaring bonfire. Many cried as they read their letters aloud, and then ceremoniously tossed them into the fire. This process enabled the participants to acknowledge their emotions and let them go.

I was so impressed by the results of this exercise. Why not try a simplified version?

Write down the names of all of the people in your life who you feel have let you down or cheated you in some way. Don't hold back. Let out your true feelings. Now take that piece of paper (maybe yours is a novel) and burn it. This symbolic exercise can be very freeing.

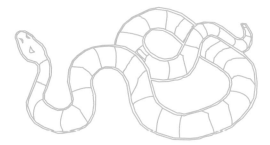

**Just as a snake sheds its skin,
we must shed our past—over and over again.**
—*Buddha*

He who conquers his anger has conquered an enemy.
—*Unknown*

The heart is like a garden.
It can grow...Compassion or fear...Resentment or
love...What seeds will you plant there?
—*Buddha*

Reflect on your present blessings,
of which every man has many: not on your past
misfortunes, of which all men have some.
—*Charles Dickens*

None of us can control what life will present us—so our most important tool is our ability to let go of our demons—those preconceived expectations that stand in the way of our being able to accept and appreciate life's beauty. To let go of our fears, we need faith. Faith is said to be detaching yourself from the outcome so that you may let whatever life is presenting unfold. When you let go of these emotions that you feel you must have, you will feel a newfound freedom. Freedom to live your life, to open your heart, to forgive and release the heaviness that weighs you down, and to unleash the fears which hold you back. You will be given back your power, you will own the rights to your own story.

Let go. Instead of losing control, you will gain control.

Learning to live is learning to let go.
—*Sogyal Rimpoche*

**Always forgive your enemies,
nothing annoys them so much.**
—*Oscar Wilde*

My tormentor is myself left over from yesterday.
—*Deepak Chopra*

**It is only when we forget all our learning
that we begin to know.**
—*Henry David Thoreau*

JON KABAT-ZINN

We can't stop the waves, but we can learn to surf.
— Jonathan Kabat-Zinn

I was first introduced to Jon Kabat-Zinn from his book, *Where Ever You Go There You Are: Mindfulness Meditation In Every Day Life*. It speaks to those just coming to meditation for the first time as well as to long-time practitioners. He describes how the emotions we carry with us color our world, and how we can learn to let them go, so that we can better navigate life.

The phrase "letting go" has to be high in the running for New Age cliché of the century. It is overused, abused daily. Yet it is such a powerful inward maneuver that it merits looking into, cliché or no. There is something vitally important to be learned from the practice of letting go.

Letting go means just what it says. It's an invitation to cease clinging to anything – whether it be an idea, a thing, an event, a particular time, or view, or desire.

But it's not only holding on with our hands. We hold on with our minds to narrow views, to self-serving hopes and wishes. Letting go really refers to choosing to become transparent to the strong pull of our own likes and dislikes, and of the unawareness that draws us to cling to them.

Letting go is only possible if we allow ourselves to recognize the lenses we slip so unconsciously between observer and observed that then filter and color, bend and shape our view.

Our mind is constantly evaluating our experiences, comparing them with other experiences or holding them up against expectations and standards that we create, often out of fear. Fear that I'm not good enough, that bad things will happen, that good things won't last, that other people might hurt me, that I won't get my way, that only I know anything, that I'm the only one who doesn't know anything.

While our thinking colors all our experience, more often than not our thoughts tend to be less than completely accurate. Usually they are

merely uninformed private opinions, reactions and prejudices based on limited knowledge and influenced primarily by our past conditioning. All the same, when not recognized as such and named, our thinking can prevent us from seeing clearly in the present moment. We get caught up in thinking we know what we are seeing and feeling. Just being familiar with this deeply entrenched pattern and watching it as it happens can lead to greater nonjudgmental receptivity and acceptance.

**In spite of everything,
I still believe that people are really good at heart.**
—*Anne Frank (1929–1945)*

Be Bold in What You Stand For, Careful in What You Fall For

Nothing makes it easier to resist temptation
than a proper bringing up,
a sound set of values, and witnesses.
—Franklin P. Jones

*T*he reputation of a lifetime may be determined by the conduct of a single moment. We are all familiar with that tiny tug of shame at our innermost muscles—our integrity muscles. When we give in, we lose just a little bit of the control we have over those muscles. Over the years, if those muscles become looser, so can our morals...and thus our reputation.

Keep your mouth shut when you are swimming
and when you are angry.
—Unknown

Talking is like playing on the harp;
there is as much in laying the hand on the strings
to stop their vibration as in twanging them
to bring out their music.
—*Oliver Wendell Holmes*

To respond immediately to an angry person is
like throwing fuel on a fire.
—*Unknown*

Never were truer words said. Of course my parents said it this way, "If you can't say anything nice, don't say anything at all." Now I might have snickered at that thought, except that my mother followed it up with another bit of wisdom, "Kill 'em with kindness. Nothing will bother them more." OK mom!

Few things are harder to put up with than
annoyance of a good example.
—*Mark Twain*

To belittle is to be little.
—*Unknown*

**There is no pillow so soft
as a clear conscience.**
—*French proverb*

When searching for our grace and dignity in challenging times, I will defer to Shakespeare's eloquent advice: "Go to your bosom; Knock there, and ask your heart what it doth know." What Will is trying to say is to look inside yourself before you speak. Anger and revenge take a physical and emotional toll on your body and soul, and they don't always elicit the best results.

**One who throws mud
gets himself soiled as well.**
—*Unknown*

**You cannot shake hands
with a clenched fist.**
—*Indira Gandhi*

Just because you need
to doesn't mean you have to.
—*Unknown*

Everything that irritates us about others can
lead us to an understanding of ourselves.
—*Carl Jung*

One thing I've found helpful is remembering that it is not another person's words or actions that cause our pain and anger, but rather the meanings and judgments that we assign to others' behaviors that cause our anguish. So before we speak or act, it is better to stop and ask ourselves, "Are we going to create anger and unhappiness or are we going to promote peace and understanding?" It is our choice how we react. And it is usually the reply that causes the trouble. The next time someone pushes your buttons, try not to listen to your ego—try not to fight back. Grace can enter our souls only when we stop trying to control the uncontrollable—nature and others. We must also remember that we are only in control of how we respond to the behavior of others, and not how well or poorly others behave.

If you are patient in one moment of anger,
you will escape many days of sorrow.

—*Unknown*

Don't let your tongue cut your throat.

—*Unknown*

Never get in a spraying contest with a skunk.

—*Unknown*

How others treat me is their path,
how I react is mine.

—*Unknown*

So how do we keep on the right path? How do we make the right choices? I'm quite a fan of Dr. Wayne Dyer. In his book, *Everyday Wisdom*, he writes, "If prayer is you talking to God, then intuition is God talking to you." We all have that inner voice. Can you hear yours? Knowing what you stand for helps that voice speak up. One of the greatest gifts in life is

discovering that we can make our own decisions, decisions that represent us and our inner selves. So it is important that we seek to find the truth about who we are, what we represent, and what we believe is right and wrong. Only then can we shape how we live our lives each day.

Lead me not into temptation:
I can find the way myself.
—*Rita Mae Brown*

Most people want to be delivered from temptation,
but would like it to keep in touch.
—*Robert Orben*

**Great minds discuss ideas,
average minds discuss events,
small minds discuss people.**
—*Hyman Rickover*

I'm reminded of a story I once read about the spiritual leader Mahatma Gandhi. Once, while his train was pulling slowly out of a station, a European reporter ran up to his compartment window. "Do you have a message I can take back to my people?" he asked. It was Gandhi's day of silence, so he searched for piece of paper upon which he wrote, "My life is my message."

What messages are we sending? We will be tested again and again, not to mention tempted. We will each choose whether to listen to that inner voice. I personally like to keep another voice around, just in case mine is too distracted by the temptation at hand to remember to speak up. I call this voice my guardian angel—that secret savior who can gently remind me when I'm about to go astray.

**Reputation is character
minus what you've been caught doing.**
—*Michael Lapoce,* **A Funny Thing Happened on the
Way to the Boardroom**

Man always travels along precipices...
His truest obligation is to keep his balance.
—*Pope John Paul II*

Wherever you are to do a thing,
though it can never be known but to yourself,
ask yourself how you would act would
all the world looking at you, and act accordingly.
—*Thomas Jefferson*

Jeff strives to instill in his campers a sense of
integrity, compassion, self reliance and fair play.

My husband, Jeff Konigsberg, runs a summer camp for children. Early in the summer, as the counselors arrive for training, he speaks not only about how to teach basketball or baseball but also how to deal with an unruly child or settle a dispute. Many times, I've heard him say, "always think about how you would react if that child's parents were looking over your shoulder." Jeff grew up hearing this philosophy from his father, Donnie, who always said, "go through life as if the person you love most is looking over your shoulder." Think about who you would choose to have looking over your shoulder. It doesn't matter whether you team up with someone alive or someone who's passed away; it just helps if you have a strong defense team. (My late father is who I always envision.)

Here's a good exercise for your "team." It's from author and speaker Stephen Covey. Close your eyes and imagine yourself at your own funeral. Here come your colleagues from your office. They're standing over you. What are they saying about you? What would you like them to be saying about you?

- ○ What reputation are you enjoying as the people pass by and look down at you?
- ○ Now here come your neighbors and friends. Are they fondly remembering your kindness and dedication in life or do you think they're worried about where you're heading now?
- ○ Finally, here comes your family. What are they recalling about your life, your relationships with each of them? Are those whom you love proud of how you'll be remembered?

This is a sobering exercise to return to now and then. You might call it a wake-up call (and God only knows you'll want to wake up from this exercise). It's never too late to start building that reputation for which you'd like to be remembered.

**What you are is God's gift to you,
and what you do with what you are is your gift to God.**
—*George Foster*

**The secret of being a bore
is to tell everything.**
—*Voltaire*

**The person who is wrapped up in himself
is generally overdressed.**
—*Unknown*

Not too long ago, I received one of those chain e-mails in my office. Probably thousands of others have received it as well. But I loved it, so I printed it out, and I've been carrying it in my wallet ever since. I thought I'd share it with you here, while you're thinking about what's really important.

○ Name the five wealthiest people in the world.

○ Name the last five Heisman trophy winners.

○ Name the last five winners of the Miss America contest.

○ Name 10 people who have won the Nobel or Pulitzer Prize.

○ Name the last dozen Academy Award winners for best actor or actress.

○ Name the last decade's worth of World Series winners.

How'd you do?

The point is, none of us remembers the headlines of yesterday. These are no second-rate achievers. They are the best in their fields. But the applause dies. Awards tarnish. Achievements are forgotten. Accolades and certificates are buried with their owners.

Here's another one: See how you do on this one:

○ List a few teachers who aided your journey through school.

○ Name three friends who have helped you through a difficult time.

○ Name five people who have taught you something worthwhile.

○ Think of a few people who have made you feel appreciated and special. Think of five people you enjoy spending time with. Name a half a dozen heroes whose stories have inspired you.

Easier?

The lesson?

The people who make a difference in your life are not the ones with the most credentials, the most money, or the most awards. They are the ones who care. They have been very successful in their lives. Their awards are in our hearts.

What we must decide is perhaps how we are valuable, rather than how valuable we are.
—*Edgar Z. Friedenber*

So how do we begin to become the person that we want to be? How do we stop letting our emotions get the best of us? How do we learn to take a step back? Interestingly, do you remember your mom ever giving you a time-out? Parents use this tool to allow their children the opportunity to reflect on a situation and hopefully learn from it. Adults could also use a time-out because it gives us the ability to assess our choices and think about what will serve us best in the end. In this way, we can respond intelligently, rather than react emotionally.

Wise men say nothing in dangerous times.
—*Unknown*

**God gave us two eyes, two ears and only one mouth.
And we should use them in that ratio.**
—*Unknown*

**Never insult an alligator
until you've crossed the river.**
—*Cordell Hull*

You've probably heard it before, "Don't burn bridges. You never know how many times you'll have to cross the same river." How many times has each of us later regretted leaving a situation on bad terms? I remember when I was just starting in news, and I was working at WABC-TV. Being the youngest reporter and "last one hired," I always got the earliest assignments in the morning and had to work weekends. I also got sent on every fire and every dead body under a bridge. One day, I returned from a story about an old lady who was being evicted because she adopted stray cats—88 of them to be exact—all living in the one-bed-room apartment where we conducted the interview. I expressed my opinion on how unfair I felt the distribution of stories was among the reporters. I felt better after I let my frustration out to this junior story assignment editor. But on my way back to my cubicle, one of the veteran reporters smiled and said, "always remember, the toes you step on today are connected to the ass you'll kiss tomorrow." Okay, so maybe I could have gotten my point across a bit more graciously. Acting with grace and dignity enables us to leave a good impression, and it's *always* best to leave a good impression, whether in your personal or business life. (By the way, that junior assignment editor became the news director.)

> **The words you speak today should be soft**
> **and tender...for tomorrow you may have to eat them.**
> **—*Unknown***

If you wouldn't write it and sign it, don't say it.
—*Earl Wilson*

Before you start on the road to revenge,
dig two graves.
—*Chinese proverb*

There is more to knowing than just being correct.
—*Benjamin Huff*

When you judge others,
you define yourself.
—*Unknown*

Put a Little Love in Your Life

We are shaped and fashioned by what we love.
—Goethe

I remember growing up, my mom always said, "Half the fun of doing anything is sharing it with others." It's so true. Friends and mates allow us to savor our successes and our joys, comfort us in our challenging moments, and provide a mirror for us to learn more about ourselves. I've always looked at friends as the family we choose. They enrich our lives. Like Robert Louis Stevenson said, "A friend is a gift you give yourself."

**A friend may well be reckoned
the masterpiece of nature.**
—*Ralph Waldo Emerson*

The most called-upon prerequisite of a friend
is an accessible ear.
—*Maya Angelou* From The Heart of a Woman

Conversely, to be a good friend or mate, I've found it's important to practice being a better listener. This means listening to
what the friend or mate says, rather than jumping to conclusions
or getting defensive. Sometimes it helps by being their "mirror"
for when they hear their words repeated back to them, it can
help them realize that what they said was not exactly what they
meant to say.

STAY is a charming word in a friend's vocabulary.
—*Louisa May Alcott*

Our own rough edges become smooth
as we help a friend smooth her edges.
—*Sue Atchley Ebaugh*

There are two ways of spreading light.
To be the candle or the mirror that reflects it.
—*Edith Wharton*

Patience, compassion, and empathy are also important traits in being a good friend or mate. You know the old golden rule, "Care for others the way you would like them to care for you." The support of a friend during a tough time could make the difference between success and failure. Encouragement and confidence are priceless gifts that can help change a person's life.

Sorrow shared is halved and joy shared is doubled.
—*Native American saying*

I always felt that the great high privilege, relief, and comfort of friendship was that one had to explain nothing.
—*Katherine Mansfield*

Treat your friends as you do your pictures, and place them in their best light.
—*Jennie Jerome Churchill*

Take care, though, with whom you choose to have these close relationships, for they have a tremendous impact on our self-esteem and our life path. As someone once told me, "The attitudes of your friends are like the buttons on an elevator. They will either take you up or they will take you down."

Keep away from people who try to belittle your ambitions. Small people always do that, but the really great make you feel that you too can become great.
—Mark Twain

Who lies with dogs rises with fleas.
—Unknown

Lots of people want to ride with you in the limo, but what you want is someone who will take the bus with you when the limo breaks down.
—Oprah Winfrey

HELPING OTHERS

> **We make a living by what we get,
> we make a life by what we give.**
> —*Unknown*

Kindness is powerful and contagious. We should never underestimate the potential of a friendly smile, a gentle touch, or a supportive word. This simple gift could make all the difference in a friend's or even a stranger's day.

> **If I can stop one heart from breaking,
> I shall not live in vain;
> If I can ease one life the aching,
> Or cool one pain,
> Or help one fainting robin
> Into his nest again,
> I shall not live in vain.**
> —*Emily Dickinson*

You cannot hold a torch to light another's path
without brightening your own.

—*Unknown*

An effort made for the happiness of others
lifts us above ourselves.

—*Lydia M. Child*

Service is the rent that we pay for our room on earth.

—*Lord Halifax*

One day when I was visiting my daughter's school counselor, I saw a plaque on her wall. I loved its words so much that I found a piece of paper and wrote them down. I'd like to share them with you, for that's what this chapter is all about—the power of sharing.

○ Give a smile to everyone you meet. The more you smile, the more you'll receive smiles.
○ Give a kind word—you will feel kind and receive kind words.
○ Give appreciation—you will appreciate and be appreciated.

○ Give honor, credit and applause—you will be honored and receive credit and applause.

○ Give time for a worthy cause—you will be worthy, and richly rewarded.

○ Give hope—you will have hope and be made hopeful.

○ Give happiness—you will be happy and be encouraged.

○ Give cheer—the verbal sunshine—you will be cheerful.

○ Give a pleasant response—you will be pleasant and receive pleasant responses.

I can't think of anything more appropriate for a guidance counselor to have so prominently displayed in an office where teenagers will come for advice. Perhaps my daughter Lindsay had soaked up these words because only a few days earlier she had commented to me, "It's nice to be important, but it's more important to be nice."

But even the sweetest of teenagers stake their claim to their own independence. And while as parents, we want to help them spread their wings, sometimes this natural process can seem like such a struggle. Lindsay was asked to write a sonnet for her 11th grade Renaissance Literature class, she chose this very subject.

Lindsay and Sarah
make each other smile

Sonnet to my mother

Mother tiger, you envelop wee me
Determinedly dragging deer down to den
Soft paw on me, fierce claw to enemy
Teaching me to hunt, time and time again
Cub hunts next with pack, mother prowls alone
Elude hyenas, at teen tiger tricks
No longer home with forlorn lonesome Joan
And for now at the hairless air she licks
Not keeping cub curfew draws a harsh roar
Daughter's claws flash, not intending to slash
But claws can't cuddle when cubs become sore
To tigress I turn when my world goes crash
Struggling to shares stripes connects us as one
Strutting from black night to luminous sun

—Lindsay L. Krauss

Guard well within yourself that treasure, kindness.
Know how to give without hesitation,
how to lose without regret,
how to acquire without meanness.
—*George Sand*

Criticism, like rain, should be gentle enough to
nourish a man's growth without destroying his roots.
—*Frank A. Clark*

When you are kind to someone in trouble,
you hope they'll remember and be kind to someone else.
And it'll become like a wildfire.
—*Whoopi Goldberg*

RELATIONSHIPS

After God created the world,
he made man and woman.
Then, to keep the whole thing from collapsing,
he invented humor.
—*Guillermo Mordillo*

When it comes to intimate relationships, most people put more
time and effort into deciding what kind of car or video player to
buy than they do into whom to have a relationship with. Is it any

wonder then that our relationships don't always turn out the way we want them to? Of course, I sometimes wonder whether God really meant for men and women to coexist under the same roof. Oh sure, physically we may look like two pieces of a puzzle that logically fit together. But psychologically and emotionally, we're so incredibly different that I'm sometimes amazed that we really belong to the same species.

Marrying a man is like buying something you've been admiring for a long time in a shop window. You may love it when you get it home, but it doesn't always go with everything else.
—*Jean Kerr,* **The Snake Has All The Lines**

Success in marriage does not come merely through finding the right mate, but through BEING the right mate.
—*Barnett Brickner*

Marriage is an ad-lib.
—*Steve Allen*

We also grow up with the notion that we will find the perfect mate. Confucius say, "Seek not every quality in one individual." We need to really examine this notion, thinking that we are going to find *every* quality we want and need in one person. What are the odds of that happening?! Having healthy relationships with people means loving them for who they are now, not for whom you hope they'll be tomorrow.

Love is unconditional commitment to an imperfect person.
—Unknown

Love is a fire.
But whether it is going to warm your hearth or
burn down your house, you can never tell.
—Joan Crawford

Sometimes I wonder if men and women
really suit each other.
Perhaps they should live next door
and just visit now and then.
—Katherine Hepburn

If we'd stop measuring our relationship and our mate against some unrealistic level of perfection…if we'd stop believing that somehow everyone else out there did find a perfect mate and has a perfect marriage…then we'd stop feeling like the grass is greener. When you ask someone, "How's everything?" They're going to say, "Great." They're not going to tell you about all of the idiosyncrasies of their mates that drive them crazy and about the various ways their marriage might not have lived up to their ideal.

Acceptance is one of the keys to happy relationships. Often, we don't recognize real moments of happiness in our lives because we've been expecting something different—something bigger or perhaps more dramatic. And don't forget, our mate may be measuring us against some unrealistic standard as well. And guess what? We're probably not seen as the perfect mate either—no matter how hard we think we're trying.

The only man I know who behaves sensibly
is my tailor; he takes my measures anew each time
he sees me. The rest go on with their
old measurements and expect me to fit them.
—*George Bernard Shaw*

**We all have a childhood dream that when there is love,
everything goes like silk, but the reality
is that marriage requires a lot of compromise.**
—*Raquel Welch*

**The ultimate test of a relationship is to
disagree but to hold hands.**
—*Alexandra Penney*

When Jeff and I were planning our wedding, we decided to write personal vows to each other that were read during the ceremony. Interestingly, we not only alluded to our differences but also joked about them as well. We took a light-hearted approach to our vows. Jeff couldn't help himself but to joke about the moment we met—in a deli. I'd been shopping for school clothes all day with my youngest daughter Sarah and we were exhausted. My eyes searched the menu for what I call "comfort food." There it was, a hot open-faced turkey sand-

wich with mashed potatoes and gravy! Much to my embarrassment, the sandwich was brought out just as Jeff introduced himself. This incident and the fact that Jeff's dad loves this kind of food, gave him fodder for his opening line. It brought the house down!

JEFF: *From the moment my eyes connected with yours at the Rye Ridge Deli, I knew that we were meant for each other. But then your turkey, mashed potatoes and stuffing lunch arrived and I thought perhaps you were more suited for my father. Joan, my dear, my love, you are a consistently beautiful person both inside and out, and I adore you with all my heart. Your girls—I still hold with love and laughter and I will protect them—always. I look forward to waking up to you for the rest of my life. Joan, I love you with all of my heart.*

JOAN: *Jeff, you had me before you said hello. In your thousand-watt smile, I saw all of the qualities I could ever want in a man: integrity, compassion, loyalty, and love of family. But I could never have imagined how wonderfully you would embrace my girls. You blended into our family seamlessly. And then there was that twinkle in your eye—every time you walk into a room. That combination makes me fall in love with you all over again. You truly are the love of my life.*

Jeff and I exchanged these vows at sunset in a candlelit ceremony. I was thrilled with every detail of the wedding, and no one could believe that it was planned in only one week. So many people have asked me why we got married so quickly. The truth is that we had been dating for three and a half years. So when Jeff popped the question, our ultimate goal was to be able to have a very private ceremony. In order to keep the tabloid press at bay, we decided it'd be best to plan the wedding quickly and quietly. It worked!

From the very beginning, Jeff truly embraced my girls, treating them as if they were his daughters. As a single parent, you hope and pray that you'll be able to find someone who will blend with you and your children to create a cohesive new family. I knew that my three daughters felt close to Jeff, but we were overwhelmed by their toast at our wedding. They created their

own rendition of the theme from "The Brady Bunch."

"We all know the story of a lovely lady, bringing up three very lovely girls.

None had hair of gold like their mother, yet they all demanded horses, cars, and pearls.

Now the story of a handsome fella—caring for 400 boys of his own. It was Takajo to which he was married, yet he was still alone.

Then that one day when this lady met that fella, and they knew that it was their destiny. I mean please…what else could've happened? They joined in the love shack of the Rye Ridge Deli!

So for three long years, their love and trust have flourished as the five grew together happily. Mom and Jeff, we wish you the best now…. We truly feel we're one big family."

**I always thought that marriage
was about finding the perfect match.
Now I realize it's about trying
to match the different pieces together perfectly.**

—Courteney Cox

What makes some relationships last a lifetime? It's a commitment to work together through all of life's ups and downs...and there will be ups and downs. You're not necessarily going to feel "full of love" for your mate all the time. That doesn't have to mean the relationship is in real trouble—commitment is about sticking around and trusting that those feelings will come back. One of the best pieces of advice I've ever heard is that if you share your marital gripes with your friends or families, you will have their judgments and suggestions to contend with as well. And those may be more than a relationship can withstand. The person with whom you should talk about your feelings is your mate.

**Trouble is a part of your life,
and if you don't share it,
you don't give the person who loves you enough
chance to love you enough.**
—*Dinah Shore*

**An archaeologist is the best husband a woman can have;
the older she gets the more interested he is in her.**
—*Agatha Christie*

Your partnership will dim and brighten with life's passages: from postpartum depression to parenting teenagers—from mid-life crises to loss of jobs and loved ones. Keeping the magic alive in your relationship means learning how to fall in love with your partner over and over again.

Husbands are like fires, they go out if unattended.
—*Zsa Zsa Gabor*

The big difference between sex for money and sex for love is that sex for money usually costs a lot less.
—*Brendan Behan*

Marriage is the only war in which you sleep with the enemy.
—*Unknown*

How can I choose a husband when I can't even decide what to wear?
—*Beth Jaylcus*

My husband said he needed more space,
so I locked him outside.
—*Roseanne Barr*

Granted, choosing the person you want to spend the rest of your life with isn't so easy. It is the ultimate commitment which will forever alter our lives. I remember reading an open letter written by Joan Rivers to her daughter, Melissa, as she was preparing for Melissa's wedding. The letter, which appeared in the November 1998 issue of *McCall's* magazine, spoke so selflessly and poignantly about the transition one makes when getting married.

Dearest darling Melissa,

I am writing this in your old room, curled up with your pink doggy, and I am crying.

I can hear you saying, "Oh, there goes my mother again!" But now I think I have a right to even more tears than I shed when you walked down the aisle to get your college diploma just nine months after daddy committed suicide. Now you are about to walk down another aisle. It is the happiest moment of your life, but Daddy isn't here to walk beside you, to give you his arm and his love, and his pride when the wedding march is played—to give you the thoughts a father gives his daughter at this momentous time. And so, with all the love that is in me, I am left to do that job solo. I will try to give you my own thoughts, which I hope will guide you. Yes, here goes your mother again, waxing mushy, as you prepare to begin your life as a wife.

As I sit here I am looking at the framed writing award won by Melissa Rosenberg in the sixth grade. I hope I can write as well now as that sixth grader did, for I am so misty with memories of you! I know, I should take my own advice and "grow up." After all, you are an adult, and you have already moved out of my house. But Missy, you'll never move out of my heart.

Remember all the needlepoint pillows I worked on so diligently when you were growing up? I took my needlepoint everywhere—to your ballet classes, your school-play rehearsals, your countless horse shows. It kept me busy and happy while I watched you being busy and happy. Each pillow reminds me of the good times I had watching you grow up, and each represents a little milestone for me.

First the pillows were just cute little pictures of clowns and balloons. Then, as you got older, they had sayings, like "Before you meet the handsome prince, you have to kiss a lot of frogs." My words of wisdom! I remember the pillow following Daddy's death the most. I made it at the end of that terrible rift between us. It said, "Welcome to Joan and Melissa's Great Adventure," and it was a symbol of the precious philosophy we formed together. We vowed that in going through life, with its good times and bad times, highs and lows, we were the stars of our own action-adventure movie. We had the power to give it a happy ending—and we would, together.

If I had time, I would needlepoint other words on pillows for you.

But instead I'll put them down on these pages, and I hope they will make your years ahead glow. These are some of the things I have learned in my life, Missy. And the lessons haven't always been easy ones, so try to listen to your mother once in a while…

BE LOYAL TO YOUR LOVE. *Daddy and I used to say that the two of us were a little army. Even before you came, he and I were shoulder to shoulder against the world. You and John must become such an army. Through the years I've always admired your loyalty to your friends, your family, your school—but the moment that ring circles your finger, your primary loyalty should be to your husband. Loyalty is the absolute essence of a marriage. John is now the most important person in your life, the one you must care about and defend and help and endlessly love. As the marriage vows say, "Forsake all others and cleave only unto your husband." Never undermine him in public or talk badly about him to anyone else. Instead, talk to each other about what bothers you, and let the world see only the colors of your strong little team.*

LEARN TO COMPROMISE. *Of course, you'll have disagreements, and you've got to air them. But never get too upset about the little things. When you were small, I used to say, "Missy, save your tears for when you are going to need them. Don't waste them on nonsense." And in marriage, so many of the things you fight over are nonsense!*

Remember when you, John and I went to look at silver patterns? Remember the couple who were actually screaming at each other over which pattern they should pick? Whatever pattern you pick, I guarantee that in six weeks you'll never notice it again. You know the last time I was aware of my silver or china pattern? When Ronald Reagan was in office!

Never fight over what's not important. Does it really matter whether the den is blue or brown? How about compromising with a plaid that has both colors? You want the bedroom warm, and he likes it cold. Okay, get an electric blanket. Be what the Japanese call the wise bamboo; in other words, learn to bend so you don't break. Be flexible, and pick your battles carefully—you'll lose nothing if you let him have his way once in a while. What gains, however, is your marriage.

And one last note on this topic: Never go to bed angry. Say what annoys you, then finish with "I love you." Trust me, it makes the morning much brighter.

Joan with her daughter Melissa and Melissa's new husband John

ENJOY THE NEW. *I don't have to tell you that really bad things happen in life. What I should add is that they happen to everyone. No one—no matter how famous or rich or brilliant—has a life without its pockets of darkness.*

When we were in the beauty salon the other day, we saw many women with perfect hair, clothes and jewels—they looked as if they had not a care in the world. But if I asked each of them, "Has there ever been a time in your life when you said, "I can't get through this; you've got to help me, God," I bet every one of them would have said yes.

So savor the happy moments as deeply as you can. Be aware—every day—of the things you and John are blessed with: youth, health, friends, family and each other. Every night in a diary, I write three good things that happened to me that day. It's a literary endeavor I strongly recommend. They can be little blessings you might often take for granted: the first snowfall of winter, when the whole world is clean and bright, and people seem so much more friendly; bumping into an old pal; having someone say "Thank you" after you've held the door open for him or her. Find delight in every day, in every way you can.

DON'T DISPLACE YOUR ANGER. *It's so easy, when things are rotten at work, when friends let you down or when you have plain old PMS, to take it out on the ones you love. Lord knows, we've done it to each other, as many mothers and daughters do. Try not to turn your anger unjustly on John—he's the one person in the world who will be the most understanding for you, the one person who can gently nudge you back into perspective. The tendency, when we feel miserable, is to* try to make others feel what we're feeling—miserable. Take a deep breath before you blow your top, and remember how much you love your husband.

MAKE YOUR MARRIAGE SIZZLE. Okay, I'm taking off my mother's hat now and putting on my girlfriend's hat. I'm not sure a mother talks to a daughter this way, but this is how I would talk to one of my closest friends who was getting married. Stay sexy—keep yourself looking attractive for your husband. Remember how you looked when you were courting? All those cute little outfits you wore, with your hair just right and your makeup perfect? Remember all those pretty panties and bras? For God's sake, don't put them in storage because you're not single anymore! Don't clod around the house in old t-shirts and torn jeans! He may be your husband, but he's your lover too. So try to fan the fires in your relationship. Be adventurous. Be flirtatious. Be aggressive!

And when the children arrive, you must try to keep taking a day or night off just for the two of you. Go to a hotel and lose yourself hopelessly in romance. There's a song that says, "How do you keep the music playing?" Missy, remember that you and John are the whole band.

KEEP LAUGHING. What better advice could a comedian-mom give you? You have always kept your sense of humor during life's darkest moments—I hope that's something you get from your mother! Remember your first prom? You were all dressed up, looking so lovely in your first strapless dress, and your date arrived wearing these hideous white cotton gloves. You rushed to your room in tears, and I went up and convinced you that white gloves were perfectly proper...for a dance at Tara! You laughed and came downstairs and told your date the joke. He laughed and removed the fashion faux pas, and off the two of you went.

A sense of humor has always helped pull me through life. It kept your dad and me going for 22 unforgettable years. It helped me handle career starts and stops, and the very unprivate life I've chosen to lead as a performer. And it will see me through this strange new position outside your life. I'm so happy for you, but I feel somewhat smaller. When I'm sad, I will think of all our happy times, our fun and silly times, these past years, Missy, and all the joy you have brought me.

We have been a great team, you and I, not merely mother and daughter, not just professional colleagues on our E! show, but devoted friends. We are two people who have flown around the world just to be together for the holidays. But now John, not I, will be your final destination. And this is right. And so I'm releasing you, my darling daughter (not that you knew I ever had to!), to go off and start your life together with John. I send you my blessings at the start of Melissa and John's Great Adventure. I love you with all my heart.

You are my heart.

First Comes Love,
Then Comes Marriage,
Then Comes Baby in a Baby Carriage

PARENTING

**There are only two lasting bequests
we can hope to give our children.
One of these is roots, the other, wings.**
—*Hodding Carter*

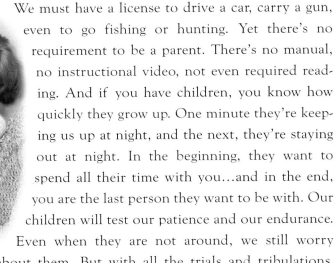

We must have a license to drive a car, carry a gun, even to go fishing or hunting. Yet there's no requirement to be a parent. There's no manual, no instructional video, not even required reading. And if you have children, you know how quickly they grow up. One minute they're keeping us up at night, and the next, they're staying out at night. In the beginning, they want to spend all their time with you...and in the end, you are the last person they want to be with. Our children will test our patience and our endurance. Even when they are not around, we still worry about them. But with all the trials and tribulations, they bring the most intense joy.

Children reinvent your world for you.
—*Susan Sarandon*

Children need love,
especially when they do not deserve it.
—*Harold S. Hulbert*

One knows one's done one's job
as a parent properly if one's
children reject everything one stands for.
—*Glenda Jackson*

Oh, to be only half as wonderful as my child
thought I was when he was small,
and only half as stupid
as my teenager now thinks I am.
—*Rebecca Richards*

We must love them, nurture them, and listen to them. In this fast-paced life we live today, we can never be too busy to give our children a hug and a kiss and let them know that no matter what happens, we'll always be there for them. When they grow up, they will remember the time we spent with them and not the gifts we bought them—so a good rule of thumb is to spend twice as much time with them and half as much money.

Your children need your presence
more than your presents.

—*Unknown*

The easiest way to convince my children
that they don't need anything is to get it for them.

—*Joan Collins*

In the final analysis it is
not what you do for your children but
what you have taught them to do for themselves that
will make them successful human beings.

—*Ann Landers*

As hard as it may be, we must let them make their own mistakes—remembering that we all learn more from our mistakes than from our successes. Maybe just as important as learning how to take care of children is learning how to let go. If only we could all remember to treasure children for who they are and not for who we want them to be. Some parents mistake parenting for cloning, and seek to make their children like themselves. Others seek to have their children fulfill the lives they never had.

Nothing has a stronger influence
physiologically on their environment,
and especially on their children,
than the unlived lives of the parents.
—*Carl Jung*

The mother who gives up her life
for her children does them no kindness, but rather
burdens them with the legacy of a life unlived.
—*Janet Faldron*

If you want to make sure
your children's feet are on the ground,
try putting some responsibility on their shoulders.
—*Unknown*

I once heard a powerful lesson in parenting delivered by Rabbi
Jon Haddon, who has presided over many Konigsberg family
events through the years. He reminded us all that parenting
should always be about nurturing our children so that they may
become independent. He drew upon the words of Israeli writer
Yehudah Amichai, "We must be careful not to protect and mold
so much that our love becomes a prison from which they must

escape. Your children are not *your* children. They are the sons and daughters of life longing for itself. They come *through* you, but not *from* you and although they are *with* you, they belong not *to* you. You may give them your love, but not your thoughts, for they have their own thoughts. You may house their bodies, but not their souls. You may strive to be like them, but seek not to make them like you."

**When we stop trying
to make our children fit our fantasies of
who they should be,
we can begin to see who they are.**
—*Unknown*

**If we try to control and hold onto our children,
we lose them. When we let them go,
they have the option of returning to us more fully.**
—*Ann Wilson Schaef*

**A mother's role is to deliver children
obstetrically once, and by car forever after.**
—*Unknown*

Celebrating with Jamie, Sarah and Lindsay

The birth of a child is truly life's greatest miracle. The joy of parenting is a gift to be savored and appreciated. I strive as a parent to "make time" so that I may appreciate the ordinary moments. I strive to marvel at their steps toward independence, rather than take offense. I strive to be more responsive and less reactive. I strive to be a more sane, peaceful person so that I set a good example. And, like all parents, I worry…and I hope that I'm doing a good job.

**The finest inheritance you can give
to a child is to allow it to make its own way,
completely on its own feet.**
—*Isadora Duncan*

As my oldest daughter Jamie "left the nest" to go off to college, I reflected on my time with her. Had I taught her everything she needed to know? Had I set the right examples? On her own, would she make the right decisions? Would she be comfortable with whom she had become? Would she have the confidence to go after her dreams? And would she remember to wash her socks and her underwear? (Some things might be too much to hope for!)

Like many parents do, once Jamie left for college, I finally felt it was safe enough to venture into her room for that spring cleaning which I'd been dying to do for 16 years! I wanted to once again be able to see the color of the carpet! As I sifted through piles, saving grammar and high school memorabilia, I came across a poem that Jamie had given me for mother's day when she was just a little girl.

Jamie at 19...highest medal-winning American at the Junior Olympics (silver and bronze)

Jamie's Poem

She's always there
To shelter me
To give me hope
To help me see
Her words are strong
And firmly spoken
But her promises
Are never broken
Through the good times
She was there
And the bad
She helped bear
Her heart is gentle
Caring and warm
Whenever I was hurt
She cried too
And whenever I ride well
Her pride shone through
Her love was never silent or restrained
And though life was hard
The good remained to help me and my sisters
My special friend
My mother

Although there are many trial marriages…
there is no such thing as a trial child.
—*Gail Sheehy*

Nothing is so potent as
the silent influence of a good example.
—*James Kent*

There are three ways to get something done:
do it yourself,
hire someone, or
forbid your kids to do it.
—*Unknown*

Nothing will bring you more joy or challenge you more than being a parent. I think if I had to pick out one of the most important qualities to hold close to our hearts as our children grow up, it would be a sense of humor. With that in mind, enjoy the following quotes.

If you don't want your children
to hear what you're saying,
pretend you're talking to them.
—E.C. McKenzie

You have a wonderful child.
Then, when he's thirteen, gremlins carry him away
and leave in his place a stranger
who gives you not a moment's peace.
—Jill Eikenberry

The thing about having a baby is that
thereafter you have it.
—Jean Kerr

We had bad luck with our kids....
They've all grown up.
—Unknown

Children have never been good at listening to their elders,
but they have never failed to imitate them.
—James Baldwin

Cleaning your house
while your kids are still growing is like shoveling
the walk before it stops snowing.
—*Phyllis Diller*

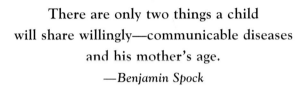

There are only two things a child
will share willingly—communicable diseases
and his mother's age.
—*Benjamin Spock*

Be nice to your children,
for they will choose your rest home.
—*Phyllis Diller*

For Fast Acting Relief, Try Slowing Down!

There must be more to life than increasing its speed.
—Mahatma Gandhi

You know how it feels when you have a million things on your mind? Your breath becomes short. Your body grows tense. Thoughts of the office, the bills, the children, the groceries you still need to pick up…all invade your head. In no time, your mind begins to spin out of control.

Although the days are jam packed with activities, we always seem to be able to squeeze in one more thing: an errand, a lunch date, a business meeting….But how many of us squeeze "ourselves" into our days. Why do "we" always get knocked off our "to do" list?

If we took better care of ourselves, we would be better mates, better parents, better friends, and better workers. Rest, relaxation, play, and reflection are vital to our overall well being. Taking a time-out means making an investment in yourself. The investment you make in yourself today will determine the quality of your life in the days and years to come.

When you feel tired, frazzled, stressed, or overwhelmed, it's important to stop and refresh your spirit and nurture your body. It doesn't matter whether you take a walk, go to a movie, listen to music, or immerse yourself in your favorite hobby. During a "time-out," you'll rekindle your spirit and perhaps even receive some important insights.

If perhaps you feel you're not in need of this kind of "time-out," please take a moment to consider how you would answer the following questions:

- ○ Do you feel tired in the morning even after you've had a "good night's sleep?"
- ○ Do you often feel like you're running out of energy when you're not even halfway through the day?
- ○ Do you have a hard time concentrating on any one activity?
- ○ Are you often irritable? Annoyed? Impatient?
- ○ Are you often feeling so overwhelmed that you can't even accomplish the simplest tasks?
- ○ Do you often snap at your colleagues, friends, or family?
- ○ Do you feel there are never enough hours in the day?

If you answered "yes" to any of the previous questions, you need to make time for yourself in your busy schedule. It's time to learn about the three R's: rest, refresh, and rejuvenate.

**The time to relax is
when you don't have time for it.**
—*Sydney J. Harris*

**Don't deny yourself a sense of play—a chance
to step down, relax, refresh yourself, put your molehills
in perspective and not let them become mountains.**
—*Unknown*

**Always leave enough time in your life to do
something that makes you happy, satisfied, even joyous.
That has more effect on economic well-being
than any other single factor.**
—*Paul Hawken*

Every coach knows the importance of resting the team before its next big game so that the players will be physically renewed. The President of the United States retreats regularly at Camp David to remain mentally alert. Even Albert Einstein and Thomas Edison were known for taking catnaps in the middle of their experiments so that they could return with more powerful insight....And for heaven's sake, even God knew enough to rest on the seventh day! (If the creator of the universe could take a day off to rest, certainly you and I can.)

**A small period of solitude
each day is remarkably healing.**
—*Unknown*

**Within you there is a stillness and sanctuary
to which you can retreat at any time and be yourself.
This sanctuary is a simple awareness of comfort,
which can't be violated by the turmoil of events.
This place feels no trauma and stores no hurt.
It is the healing mental space
that one seeks to find in meditation.**
—*Hermann Hesse*, Siddharta

**The enlightened man eats
when he is hungry and sleeps when he is tired.**
—*Zen saying*

I used to live my life in a much more frenzied way—always try-ing to keep up—always planning what I had to do next. It was almost like being propelled forward by a force bigger than me. If you've ever been caught in a huge crowd, where you are literally swept along by its forward movement, you know what I mean. As a reporter, I covered enough New York City demonstrations to know this helpless, frightening feeling.

It's easy to get caught up in the momentum of life. All too often, when I tried to slow down and make time for myself, I would be fraught with feelings of guilt. Surely this meant I was taking time away from my children, my spouse, or my work. How could I be so *selfish* or *lazy*?

If you find that you are overwhelmed with responsibilities to the point of mild insanity, learn to give yourself a "time-out." Notice I didn't say *treat* yourself. Giving yourself a break is not a treat—it's a vital necessity to your well-being.

**In the name of God,
stop a moment, close your work,
and look around you.**

—*Leo Tolstoy*

Know the true value of time;
snatch, seize, and enjoy every moment of it.
—*Lord Chesterfield*

Every now and then go away,
have a little relaxation, for when you come back
to your work your judgement will be surer;
since to remain constantly at work will cause you to
lose power of judgement....Go some distance away,
because the work appears smaller, and
more of it can be taken in at a glance, and a
lack of harmony or proportion is more readily seen.
—*Leonardo DaVinci*

IF YOU HAD AN EXTRA HOUR IN YOUR DAY, HOW WOULD YOU
SPEND IT? (Cleaning out closets, filing, and paying bills are not
acceptable!) Think about those things that would make you feel
more rested and less stressed.

I asked the people who work with me how they would answer

this question.

Jill Seigerman, production supervisor and new
mother: "Lying on a lounge in a pool, on a hot,
sunny day in the country, listening only to the
sounds of nature."

Lori Bzura, production manager and new wife: "Lying on a beautiful beach with my husband at 5 p.m., my favorite time of the day."

Alissa Mazer, personal assistant and single New Yorker: "Definitely a bath...I'm very into taking baths...bath beads, bubbles, and candles—that'd be perfect."

Linda Meyer, television writer/producer and mother of two: "Sitting out in my backyard, at six in the morning, reading the *Sunday Times* with a cup of coffee."

Kristen Barry, hair stylist, engaged to be married: "Hanging out at a stable with my horse, Fiona, riding and grooming her."

❍ When was the last time you took some time off from your daily routine?

❍ When was the last time you had some quiet time with yourself?

❍ When was the last time you watched the sunset?

❍ When was the last time you took a leisurely drive with your mate or a friend?

❍ When was the last time you took a long, luxurious nap?

Slow down, you move too fast.
You got to make the morning last.
—*Paul Simon and Art Garfunkel*

Learning the truth about the value of relaxation and reflection didn't happen overnight, but I did learn. I've made the effort to take the frenzy and sense of emergency out of my daily life. I've made the effort to put playfulness, serenity, and, dare I say, even laziness into my life. I consider the latter the most luxurious and definitely the most difficult. But I highly recommend trying it.

What we cultivate in times of ease,
we gather as strength for times of change.
—*Buddha*

Retreat can move you forward.
—*Unknown*

**True silence is the rest of the mind:
it is to the spirit what sleep is to the body,
nourishment and refreshment.**
—*William Penn*

Slowing down to the "speed of life" has allowed me to enjoy each day so much more. Self-reflection has given me the opportunity to tap into my deeper self and, in the end, become much more productive. Someone once likened these self-nurturing breaks to the emergency instructions we're given on an airplane. The flight attendants always tell us to put on our own oxygen masks before helping our children. Why? Because we need to help ourselves first so that we'll be better equipped to help others. In the same way, tending to ourselves will leave us better equipped to help others.

**Your vision will become clear only
when you can look into your own heart.
Who looks outside, dreams;
Who looks inside, awakens.**
—*Carl Jung*

**Plenty of people miss their share of happiness,
not because they never found it,
but because they didn't stop to enjoy it.**
—*W. Feather*

The hardest work of all is to do nothing.
—*Jewish saying*

List five things you'd love to do for yourself—to nourish your mind and body—but think you don't have the time to do. Now imagine how you would rearrange your schedule to include even one of those things:

My list used to look like this:

○ GET PHYSICAL—I learned that if I want to have an active, exciting life in decades to come, I better make the investment in my physical well-being today. So I began making appointments with myself. I gave my commitment to my health the same importance as my commitment to my family or my boss. Even if you only have 15 or 20 minutes in a day to work out, that's better than no activity at all.

○ MEDITATE—In the midst of a tornado lies a tranquil center. We can use that metaphor in our busy, frenzied, overscheduled lives. It has been a long process for me to learn to be disciplined enough to incorporate this into my life, and daring enough to settle in with my own thoughts. Just like exercise, even if I only have a few minutes, I find a quiet place to sit and let my mind and my soul rest and rejuvenate.

○ TAKE LONG BATHS—Although I've always considered long, bubbly, candlelit baths the ultimate luxury, for years I never took the time to enjoy them. But when I finally allowed myself to indulge, I learned how much I really needed this kind of self-nurturing.

○ PAMPER MYSELF—Even though I interviewed beauty experts for years on the importance of caring for your skin, I was moving too fast to take the time to lather my body in hydrating lotion, much less deep clean with a facial mask! Believe it or not, despite spending all of those years in front of the camera, I never took the time to pamper myself. These days my mantra is, "If you let your body wear out, you won't have any place to live."

○ BE BORED—As a child, being bored is the worst possible fate. If only we knew that when we grew up it would be the most sought-after luxury! Ahh—to be bored—and then afterwards—to rest. Last summer, for the first time in my life, I let myself enjoy time. I had never approached down time in this way before, and I didn't know how to welcome it. I actually used to get edgy, sitting next to the lake, just taking in its beauty; I always felt like I should be doing a million other things. Now I revel in moments like that.

Be mindful of how you approach time.
Watching the clock is not the same as watching the sunset.
—*The Key To Life*

As you become more comfortable with your time-out, I highly recommend you begin some form of meditation. It is a powerful tool that will help you relax, resolve mental tensions, and cope more effectively with stress. The mind and body are so completely interlinked that we now know physical training will keep us mentally alert, and, conversely, meditation can enhance our physical health and performance.

Meditation is not an evasion,
it is a serene encounter with reality.
—*Thich Nhat Hanh*

When you don't talk, you hear yourself better.
—*Unknown*

Like water which can clearly mirror the sky and the trees
only so long as its surface is undisturbed,
the mind can only reflect the true image of the self
when it is tranquil and wholly relaxed.
—*Indra Devi*

We live in a society obsessed with productivity. However, studies show that meditation actually increases creativity as well as productivity. And businesses which have incorporated meditation into the work lives of their executives report improved concentration and decision-making skills. Effective resting is an art that many successful people have mastered.

The mind is like a pond.
On the surface you see all the disturbances.
Yet the surface is only a fraction of the pond.
It is in the depth below the surface,
where there is stillness that you will come to know the
true essence of the pond, as well as your own mind.
—*Dr. Wayne W. Dyer*

There are many forms of meditation—take the time to read about them and find one which makes you feel comfortable. Whatever style you choose, this form of "relaxed attentiveness" will help you be in touch with your inner responses to the world around you.

While I'm not an expert on meditation, I thought you might appreciate these basic tips.

- ○ If you meditate while lying down, you'll likely fall asleep...(not necessarily a bad thing if you're exhausted and sleep deprived, but you miss that appointment with your inner self).
- ○ If you meditate in the bathtub (I love lighting lots of white candles and soothing music), you'll get wrinkly skin.
- ○ If you take a strolling meditation (I've only tried this once, and was too distracted and nervous I'd fall on my face), watch your step.

I was first introduced to the concept of meditation by reading Deepak Chopra's books. As soon as I learned how meditation could so enhance my mind and body—my emotional tranquility, my physical well-being, and my mental clarity—I was hooked. Yet it took me a long time to gather up the courage to begin meditation classes because the art of quieting the mind seemed so foreign to me. I asked Deepak Chopra to share some meditation exercises for this chapter. I trust you'll really enjoy them.

DEEPAK CHOPRA

**Health is not just the absence of a disease.
It's an inner joyfulness that should be ours all the time,
a state of positive well-being.**
—*Deepak Chopra,* Journey Into Healing

BREATH AWARENESS MEDITATION

Close your eyes and take a slow deep breath. Now exhale completely, releasing all the tension from your body. With each outflow of your breath, allow your muscles to relax. Bring your attention into your neck and shoulders and relax them with your next exhalation. Feel the tension flowing out of your upper arms...forearms...wrists...and fingers. Release the tightness from your hips...thighs...and calves. Now soften the muscles of your upper...and lower back. Enjoy this state of deep relaxation and comfort.

Now simply become aware of your breathing. Observe the inflow and outflow of your breath without trying to change it any way. With no effort on your part you may notice that your breathing changes. It may become deeper...or more shallow. It may change in its rate or rhythm. It may even seem to pause for a time. Allow whatever changes you notice to occur without any resistance. Simply observe your breath with an attitude of acceptance and innocence.

You may notice that at times your attention drifts away to a thought in your mind...a sensation in your body...or a sound in the environment. It's fine. Whenever you notice that your attention has drifted away from your breathing, very gently bring it back to your breath, in a very effortless manner.

Continue like this for the next ten minutes, then whenever you are ready, open your eyes slowly.

VIBRATING LIGHT

Take a deep breath and hold it for a moment. As you exhale, make a very soft humming sound, audible only to you. Feel the vibration in your throat and chest and allow it to center you. Repeat this a few more times, creating a soft, soothing vibration.

Now, this time as you exhale, imagine you are generating a warm golden light in the same spot as the vibration you are making. With each outflow of your breath, this warm, calming light becomes brighter. It expands into your chest and neck, carrying its soothing influence into your body and mind. This calming light encompasses your belly...your arms...your legs...your entire body. It infuses every tissue and every cell in your body with warm, peaceful, comfort-

able energy. It makes you feel completely safe and secure. Any tension you may be holding melts away under the calming influence of this gentle light. Enjoy the sensation of total comfort.

Now slowly bring the light back into your chest as you again focus your attention on a soft vibration that you generate with each outflow of your breath. Continue like this for several more breaths. When you are ready, open your eyes slowly.

HEART MEDITATION

Close your eyes and take a deep slow breath. Slowly exhale, releasing any tension you may be holding in your body. Now bring your attention into the area of your heart. For a few moments, simply be with the sensations you are carrying in your heart.

Now consider all the things for which you are grateful. Acknowledge everything in your life for which you feel gratitude.

Now take a few moments to relinquish any grievances, regrets, or hostility you may be holding. Simply have the intention to release all feelings that are not nourishing your heart.

With your attention in your chest, see if you can perceive the throbbing of your heartbeat, either as a sensation or subtle vibration. Now have the intention for your heartbeat to slow down...slow down...slow down.

Now shift your attention into your hands and become aware of your heartbeat in your hands. Have the intention to increase the blood flow and warmth to your hands.

Now direct your attention to any part of your body that you believe needs healing and feel your heart throbbing in that area. If there is no place in your body that needs attention, simply be aware of your heart throbbing in your chest. Enjoy this deep state of relaxation in body and mind.

Whenever you are ready, bring your attention back to this time and place, while you continue to feel very comfortable and fully relaxed.

NATURAL BEAUTY

Close your eyes and take a few slow deep breaths. With each inflow and outflow of your breath, allow yourself to become more relaxed...more comfortable...more peaceful. As you drift into a deep state of relaxation, imagine that you are transported to a beautiful, serene, natural environment. The air is warm and fragrant with the aroma of sweet, tropical flowers. The sky is deep blue with only a rare billowy cloud lazily floating by. The sun bathes you in its comforting, warm light. The sounds of exotic bird songs and the whisper of a soft breeze through the trees offer a soothing auditory background.

In this beautiful place, imagine yourself lying on a blanket on a soft grassy mound. Feel the sense of comfort and connection as you allow the nurturing sounds, sensations, sights, and smells

to comfort you. Enjoy this experience of being embraced by Mother Nature.

When you are ready, slowly orient yourself back to this place and time. Carry your feelings of comfort and relaxation with you.

ABOVE THE CLOUDS

Close your eyes, take a deep breath and release it, allowing all the tension in your body to flow out with your exhalation. Repeat this process a few more times, allowing your body to relax deeply. Now imagine that you are embarking on a magical hot air balloon ride. The craft that will be carrying you is absolutely safe and the weather is perfect for a gentle journey. Your guide is highly qualified and experienced so your only job is to relax and enjoy the ride.

The brightly colored balloon effortlessly lifts you off the ground as you behold the beautiful landscape below you. Lush green rolling hills unfold beneath you. Majestic treetops are just beyond your reach as you quietly float above them. Ranging sheep, oblivious to your presence, leisurely graze on the rich grasslands. A gentle mountain stream meanders through the luxuriant valleys.

Continue observing the scenes unfolding underneath you, noticing how lovely and joyful the world looks from this perspective. With just your intention, you can direct the balloon to travel any place you choose. Explore this enchanting place for a while.

Whenever you are ready, bring yourself back with a very gentle landing to this time and place.

SPROUTING

Close your eyes, take a full deep breath and release it slowly, allowing the tension in your body to flow out of you. With each inflow envision nourishing, inspiring life force filling your body. And with each out-flow of your breath, continue releasing any tension, fear or discomfort you may be holding as you find yourself becoming increasingly com-fortable, peaceful and open to life-affirming transformation.

Now imagine that you are transported to a beautiful beach on a warm summer day. You hear the sounds of seagulls calling to the waves while you lie on a blan-ket over the soft sand, pro-tected from the direct rays of the sun by a woven umbrella.

Feel the support of Mother Earth, uphold-ing you with her sweet strength and stability. Imagine deep, unwavering energy flowing from the heart of the earth, through the sand into your body, infusing you. Feel yourself becoming grounded in the vitality of the earth.

Now allow your attention to go to the sun, the source of all life energy. Bring the golden energy of the sun down into your body, into your heart. Feel your connection with the sun as it nurtures and enlivens you. Observe the intermingling of the earth's supporting energy rising up to nourish you and the radiating vitality of the sun bathing you in its life giving energy. Enjoy the dance of Mother Earth and Father Sun as they rejoice in your being.

Whenever you feel ready, return your attention to this place and time and slowly open your eyes.

PLAYGROUND

Close your eyes, take a deep breath and recall or imagine a time as a young child when you were taken to the playground at a park by your parent or caregiver. As soon as you noticed the slide and swings, your enthusiasm wells up in you and you could hardly wait to start playing.

You race over to the swing set, where you are lifted up so you may have a firm seat, holding tightly onto the chains. You ask for a push and in a moment you are soaring high up above the sand, reveling in sensations of lightness and liberation. With every gentle shove you swing higher, soon towering over the children playing in the sandbox. You are fully absorbed in the moment of playfulness.

When you have had your fill of swing, dash over to the slide. Envision yourself climbing to the top of the slide, holding onto the railing as you ascend one leg after the other. Carefully maneuvering into a sitting position, you cast off and feel the exhilaration of sliding down into the waiting arms of your parent or caregiver at the bottom of the slide. No sooner do you touch the ground than you race again to the stairs scrambling up for another thrilling slide down. Enjoy this sense of freedom and enthusiasm for life.

Delight in your experience, recalling the sensation of being light-hearted, carefree and in present moment awareness.

Whenever you are ready, bring your attention back to this time and place, feeling refreshed and relaxed. After a few moments, slowly open your eyes.

Age Is a State of Mind

There is a fountain of youth;
it is your mind, your talents, the creativity
you bring into your life and the
lives of people you love.
—Sophia Loren

When my daughter Jamie was about four years old, I went to her room to read her stories before going to sleep. In those days I awakened at 3:45 a.m. each morning to do "Good Morning America," so it was always a task to stay awake as I lay in bed with her each night reading her to sleep. On this particular night, I was especially tired and dozed off mid-sentence. As Jamie tried to gently shake me, I awakened and said, "I'm sorry, sweetheart, I'm just so tired, I can't keep my eyes open tonight." Jamie replied caringly, "That's OK mommy. You go lay down in your bed and let your brain rewind." My reaction at the time was that she was watching far too many videos. But it may have actually been a very astute observation of the human mind.

> **Getting older doesn't have to mean the end;**
> **these days there's no such thing as over the hill,**
> **because the hill has been moved—whether**
> **you're hitting your forties, or**
> **well into your fifties, or sixty or beyond.**
>
> —*Joan Rivers*

Deepak Chopra, in his best-selling book, *Ageless Body, Timeless Mind*, says that aging is not something that happens to us, but rather something our body has learned to do. He contends that, as children, we are fed verbal cues which run inside our heads like muffled tape loops, amounting to over 25,000 hours of pure conditioning. This conditioning then creates an inherited expectation that our body must deteriorate with time. So does our expectation create a self-fulfilling prophecy? The scientific community has dramatically modified its notions of aging over the last two decades—since no wear-and-tear theory has ever held up under scrutiny. Obviously, our time on this earth is limited, but we have a great deal of control over how long we live and how good we feel.

Follow the advice of baseball player Satchel Paige, who said, "Age is a question of mind over matter. If you don't mind, it don't matter." So the best way to age with grace is to assume we will. It's never too late to rekindle your spirit and thirst for adventure. Never stop chasing your dreams and trying new things. Understand that you must take an active role in staying young at heart.

**You can't help getting older,
but you don't have to get old.**
—*George Burns*

**Life is like riding a bicycle;
you don't fall off unless you stop pedaling.**
—*Unknown*

**You cannot control the length of your life,
but you can control its breadth, depth and height.**
—*Evan Esar*

I'd like to grow very old as slowly as possible.
—*Irene Mayer Selznick*

HAPPINESS
A KEY TO GROWING OLD GRACEFULLY

Bobby McFerrin sang, "Don't Worry, Be Happy." Richard Carlson wrote, "Don't Sweat the Small Stuff, And It's All Small Stuff." These philosophies may seem too simplistic to be realistic. But the truth is that we can all have happiness in our lives, for happiness is a choice. This is a hard concept for many of us to accept, but psychologists tell us that all emotions are choices. We choose to be angry, sad, happy, or bored.

I'll never forget the day I first heard that concept—that even boredom is a choice. At first, I found that disturbing, because it meant I had to take responsibility for my feelings and my own happiness. But I have since found it to be empowering, to know that I actually have that much control over my life.

Happiness is a thing to be practiced, like the violin.
—*John Lubbock*

The gift of happiness belongs to those who unwrap it.
—*Unknown*

The road to happiness is always under construction.
—*Brian Luke Seaward, Ph.D.*

No man is happy who does not think himself so.
—*Publius Syrus*

But how do we exercise this kind of control over our happiness? We can start by identifying which of our expectations are realistic and unrealistic. Sometimes the higher our expectations, the less we are able to appreciate what we have. I've found that, in quiet, reflective moments, if I can be truly honest and objective with myself, I can identify my expectations. For instance, I want my children to respect me during their teenage years, and maybe even spend a precious Saturday night with me now and then! Once we recognize an expectation, we can do one of three things. Meet it. Forget it. Or replace it with something more realistic. But worrying, fretting, and obsessing over it never works. As for those terrible teens, I must recognize their sometimes less than subtle quest for independence is just age-appropriate behavior. Of course it doesn't hurt to practice deep breathing, repeating the parent's mantra, "This too shall pass."

Life is ten percent what you make it,
and ninety percent how you take it.
—*Irving Berlin*

The foolish person seeks happiness in the distance.
The wise grow it under their feet.
—*James Oppenheim*

DEVELOP AN ATTITUDE OF GRATITUDE

A happy person is not a person in a certain set of circumstances but rather a person with a certain set of attitudes. It helps if every now and then we examine whether or not we have given enough importance to that which we have in our lives. It is only with an appropriate sense of gratitude that we are likely to embrace the good in our lives. These are the kinds of questions that can help us measure our happiness.

Jamie and Lindsay are grateful for their close relationship

Suffering, of course, is always an option. And I think we're all pretty good at this. Most often, we sabotage our happiness by concentrating on whatever is missing or flawed. Whenever my daughters grumble about something they don't have, I always tell them to be grateful for what they have and enjoy those things, as opposed to complaining about what they don't have. And every now and then, I even hear myself and I'm reminded to practice what I preach!

**Now is no time to think of what you do not have.
Think of what you can do with what there is.**
—*Ernest Hemingway*

What are your expectations? Are they realistic? If we want a happy ending, we need to let go of the fairy tale and start appreciating our reality.

Life itself is the proper binge.
—Julia Child

These days come and go,
but they say nothing,
and if we do not use the gifts they bring,
they carry them as silently away.
—Ralph Waldo Emerson

How we view our reality has a lot to do with our level of happiness. And if our view of life is a negative one, we're most likely discontent. In fact, studies will show that we're also more likely to be unhealthy. Negative thinking tends to create stress and unhappiness. We tend to think that it is being unhappy that leads people to complain, when actually it is complaining that leads people to become unhappy. Dissatisfaction and negative thinking become habits. But as we all know, habits can be broken.

**Life is full of misery, loneliness,
and suffering—and it's all over much too soon.**
—*Woody Allen*

**I'm not afraid to die,
I just don't want to be there when it happens.**
—*Woody Allen*

So how do we break the habit of negative thinking? Why not try the simplistic advice, "Don't Worry, Be Happy." Decide to eliminate all of your negative thoughts for one week. That's right, no worrying, stressing, or complaining. (OK—I didn't say this was going to be an easy exercise but it's definitely worthwhile.) For one week, resolve that you will stop comparing what you have right now with what you hoped you'd have. Determine that whatever your lot in life, you're building on it.

**The qualities of our later life will be
determined by the life we have already shaped.**
—*Rose Kennedy*

The best thing about the future is that
it comes only one day at a time.
—*Abraham Lincoln*

It helps to smile as you try to eliminate your negativity. I find that the physical response that comes with smiling makes the exercise so much easier. In fact, every time I speak to a group of women, I tell them that a mind lift is better than a face lift! And as long as I'll provide them with a list of the top five plastic surgeons on each coast, I can usually get them to say they'll at least try the exercise!

The broader you smile at your troubles,
the easier you can swallow them.
—*Unknown*

Wrinkles should merely indicate where smiles have been.
—*Mark Twain*

Laughter is a tranquilizer with no side effects.
—*Arnold H. Glascow*

SMILE!

IT INCREASES YOUR FACE VALUE

You are never fully dressed without a smile.
—From *Annie*

Did you know that the best prescription for beating the blues could be as simple as a smile or a laugh? According to researchers at Clark University in Worcester, Massachusetts, we should force ourselves to grin and bear it, literally. The students in the study were told to assume happy, sad, or angry facial expressions and postures for four minutes. The researchers found that the students maintained those moods for up to one hour later.

James Laird, Ph.D., Clark University Professor of Psychology and coauthor of the study, said they are not exactly sure why it happens but, "One theory is that acting happy forces your brain to evoke good memories, which in turn puts you in a better mood. Scowling, on the other hand, makes you feel angrier, by conjuring up bad memories."

People who keep stiff upper lips,
find that it's damn hard to smile.
—*Judith Guest*

Always laugh when you can.
It is cheap medicine.
—*Lord Byron*

A smile is a curve that sets everything straight.
—*Phyllis Diller*

What a wonderful life I've had....
I only wish I'd realized it sooner.
—*Colette*

Henry David Thoreau wrote, "Love your life. Accept the beauty offered you, for what it is. Don't question it. Don't analyze it." Once again, simplistic advice from a profound philosopher. But isn't he suggesting that we stop looking for someone or something to make us happy? What Thoreau implies is that happiness is a feeling, not an outcome. We don't become happy when we become successful. We become successful because we exude happiness and confidence. We don't become happy because we find a great mate. We attract a great mate because we are happy, fun-loving, comfortable people. Embracing this philosophy can be empowering and can change your perspective on happiness. How many of us are actually waiting around for someone or something to make us happy? We could wait forever for that! Our happiness resides within ourselves.

**Cheerfulness keeps up a kind of "daylight" in the mind,
and fills it with a steady and perpetual serenity.**
—*Joseph Addison*

**Life is a mirror; if you frown at it, it frowns back;
if you smile, it returns the greeting.**
—*William Thackeray*

Those Who Laugh… Last!

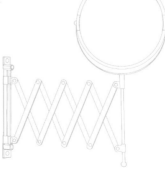

Did you know that laughter can also lower blood pressure, reduce anxiety, and give us more energy? Two minutes of hearty laughter has been likened to approximately 10 minutes on the rowing machine. That I like!

Humor therapy is actually now a growing field of medicine called psychoneuroimmunology, which is the study of the relationship between the emotional and the physical. While we've known for ages that stress weakens the body's overall condition, we are now learning that the opposite is also true: feel-good emotions have a positive impact on our health. It's been said that it's potent enough to ward off colds, stifle the flu, and help us sleep better. That's right, good old-fashioned laughter is getting a lot of attention these days for its role in boosting the immune system. In fact, it has been proven that laughter increases the production of our bodies' killer cells that attack some forms of cancer.

All this gives new meaning to the phrase "fall down laughing" for smiling and laughter seem to be the ultimate stress management technique. Researchers say we can't be physically tense if we are laughing. A good laugh provides a cathartic release, a cleansing of emotions, and a release of emotional tension. Even after the laughter has ended, body tensions continue to decrease. So the next time you're feeling sad or stressed, flash a big smile or give a hearty laugh. There's a lot of truth in the old adage, "Those who laugh…last."

A person without humor is like a
car without shock absorbers.
—*Unknown*

One loses many laughs by not laughing at oneself.
—*Sara Jeannette Dunkin*

Laughter is the brush that
sweeps away the cobwebs of the heart.
—*Mort Walker*

IT'S NEVER TOO LATE TO HAVE A HAPPY CHILDHOOD

Another secret to aging successfully is finding and following
our passions.

Interestingly, we are very good at doing this with our children. We help them find passions to keep them active, healthy,
and build self-esteem. Why would it work for them and not for
us? Whether it's tennis, golf, gardening, sailing, activism, or community charity work, keep active, keep involved, keep giving of
yourself and helping others, so that your life has purpose, vigor,
vitality, and friends.

Youth is a wonderful thing.
What a crime to waste it on children.
—*George Bernard Shaw*

I believe the second half of one's life is meant
to be better than the first half.
The first half is finding out how you do it.
And the second half is enjoying it.
—*Frances Lear*

Nothing great happens until after you're forty.
—*Coco Chanel*

When I think of what my "golden years" might be like, I envision myself playing golf in Florida, riding a bike, playing tennis, maybe even trekking the Himalayas—a life-long dream. I envision myself taking college courses and reading books I never got a chance to read because I was always so busy working. And I envision myself sitting on a beach looking out at a sunset, meditating, still learning about myself and my place in the world.

**Age is something that doesn't matter,
unless you're a cheese.**
—Billie Burke

I want to be a work in progress, always growing and always changing. You know what they say, "Keep changing. When you're through changing, you're through."

If you obey all the rules, you miss all the fun.
—Katherine Hepburn

**The secret of staying younger is to live honestly,
eat slowly, and lie about your age.**
—Lucille Ball

Big deal! I'm used to dust!
—Erma Bombeck's requested gravestone epitaph

SUGGESTIONS FOR FURTHER READING

$\mathcal{H}$ere is my "reading list" of books that have inspired me, as well as provided many of the sayings, epigrams, and words of wisdom I have collected in this book.

Mac Anderson (Editor), *The Power of Goals*, Successories, 1992

Doyle Barnett, *20 Communication Tips for Couples*, New World Library, 1995

Stefan Bechtel and Laurence Roy Stains, *The Good Luck Book*, Workman Publishing Company, 1997

Evelyn L. Beilenson, *Women*, Peter Pauper Press, 1991

Herbert Benson, M.D., *Timeless Healing: The Power of Biology and Belief*, Fireside, 1997

Terry Braverman, *When the Going Gets Tough, The Tough Lighten Up!*, Mental Floss Publications, 1997

H. Jackson Brown, Jr. Robyn Spizman, *A Hero in Every Heart*, Thomas Nelson, 1996

H. Jackson Brown, Jr., *Life's Little Instruction Book*, Rutledge Hill Press, 1992
  Life's Little Instruction Book – Volume II, Rutledge Hill Press 1993
  Life's Little Instruction Book – Volume III, Rutledge Hill Press, 1995
  Life's Little Treasure Book On Parenting, Rutledge Hill Press, 1995
  Live and Learn and Pass It On – Volume II, Rutledge Hill Press, 1996

Richard Carlson, Ph.D., *Don't sweat the small stuff...and it's all small stuff*, Hyperion, 1997

Richard Carlson and Joseph V. Bailey, *Slowing Down to the Speed of Life*, Harper San Francisco, 1998

Karen Casey, *Each Day A New Beginning*, Hazelden, 1996

Rachel Chandler, *The Most Important Lessons in Life: Letters to a Young Girl*, Element, 1998

Deepak Chopra, M.D., *Ageless Body, Timeless Mind*, Three Rivers Press, 1998

Deepak Chopra, M.D., *Journey Into Healing*, Harmony Books, 1999

Alan Cohen, *A Deep Breath of Life*, Hay House, 1996

John Coleman, *Questions From Your Cosmic Dance*, Hazeldon, 1997

Beth Mende Conny, *Inspiration for Living*, Peter Pauper Press, 1992

Valerie Coursen, *Rainbows Notes*, Running Press, 1996

Valerie Coursen, *Smiles Notes*, Running Press, 1996

Stephen R. Covey, *First Thing First Every Day*, Fireside, 1997
    The 7 Habits of Highly Effective People, Fireside, 1990

Barbara De Angelis, Ph.D., *Inspirations About Love*, Nataraj, 1996

Dr. Wayne W. Dyer, *Awakening*
    Everyday Wisdom, Hay House, 1993
    Wisdom of the Ages, HarperCollins, 1998

Eknath Easwaran, *Meditations*, Nilgiri, 1991
    Your Life is Your Message

Armand Eisen, *Believing in Ourselves*, Andrews McMeel Publishing, 1992
    The 1960s: Words of a Decade, Ariel Books

David Essel, M.S. *Phoenix Soul*, David Essel, 1998

Susan Feuer, *Success: A Book of Wit and Wisdom*, Andrews McMeel Publishing, 1995

Ruth Fishel, *Time for Joy*, Health Communications, 1989

Robert I. Fitzhenry (Editor), *The Harper Book of Quotations*, HarperCollins, 1994

Forbes Leadership Library, *Thoughts on Virtue*, Triumph Books, 1996

Don Gabor, *Big Things Happen When You Do the Little Things Right*, Prima, 1997

Cindy Garner, *How Are Men Like Noodles?*, Newport House, 1995

Melina Gerosa, *The Fun Book*, Simon & Schuster, 1998

Lori Giovannoni, *Success Redefined*, Innisfree, 1997

Kim Goad, *Magic Moments*, Commune-A-Key, 1997

Bonni Goldberg, *Room to Write*, JP Tarcher, 1996

Jennifer Habel, *For Mom*, Peter Pauper Press, 1992

Susan Hayward, *A Guide for the Advanced Soul*, Little, Brown, 1995

Napoleon Hill and Michael J. Ritt, Jr., *Napoleon Hill's Keys to Positive Thinking*, Plume, 1999

Jeanette Isabella, *Someday is Here!*, Jnetics, 1999

Tony Jeary, *A Good Sense Guide to Happiness in Your Business and Personal Life*, Trade Life, 1999

Jon Kabat-Zinn, Ph.D., *Full Catastrophe Living*, Delta, 1990 *Wherever You Go There You Are*, Hyperion, 1995

Jack Kornfield, *Buddha's Little Instruction Book*, Bantam Doubleday Dell, 1994

Ken Kragen, *Life is a Contact Sport*, William Morrow, 1994

Bruce Lansky (Editor), *Age Happens*, Meadowbrook Press, 1996

Earnie Larsen and Carol Hegarty, *Believing in Myself*, Simon & Schuster, 1992

Michael Lynberg (Editor), *A Wealth of Wisdom*, St. Martin's Press, 1996

Cynthia Walker McCullough, *My Husband Said He Needed More Space (So I Locked Him Outside)*, Fireside, 1998

John Mason, *Don't Wait For Your Ship to Come In...Swim Out to Meet It!*, Honor Books, 1994

James J. Mapes, *Quatum Leap Thinking*, Quantum Leap Thinking Organization, 1998

Ellen McGrath, Ph.D, *When Feeling Bad is Good*, Bantam,1994

Peter McWilliams, *The Portable Life 101*, Unknown, 1995

Barbara Milo Ohrbach, *All Things Are Possible—Pass The Word*, Clarkson Potter, 1995

Barbara Milo Ohrbach, *If You Think You Can...You Can!*, Clarkson Potter, 1998

J.T. O'Hara, *The Gift of Happiness Belongs to Those Who Unwrap It and Other Tidbits for Living the Good Life by One Smart Cookie*, Andrews McMeel, 1998

Debra P. Raisner, Glenn S. Klausner and David H. Raisner, *It's All Right...*, Andrews McMeel, 1996

Alexander Lockhart, *Positive Charges*, Zander Press, 1995

Susan L. Rattiner, *Women's Wit and Wisdom*, Dover, 2000

Bryan Robinson and Jamey McCullers, *611 Ways to Boost Your Self Esteem, Accept Your Love Handles and Everything About Yourself*, Health Communications, 1994

Jonathan Robinson, *Instant Insight*, Health Communications, 1996

Anthony Robbins, *Awaken the Giant Within*, Fireside, 1993

Kathleen Russell and Larry Wall, *Achieve Your Dreams*, Walrus Productions, 1994

Michael Ryan, *Hollywords*, Great Quotations, 1993

Steven S. Sadleir, *The Awakening*, Self Awareness Institute, 1993

Anne Wilson Schaef, *365 Meditations for People Who (May) Worry Too Much Meditations for Women Who Do Too Much*, Harper San Francisco, 1996

Dr. Seuss, *Seuss-isms*, Random House, 1997

Brian Luke Seaward, *Dessert is Stressed Spelled Backwards*, Conari Press, 1999 *Stand Like Mountain Flow Like Water*, Health Communications, 1997

Gary Smalley, *Forever Love: 119 Ways to Keep Your Love Alive*, World Books, 1997

Leonard Sorcher, *The Optimist See The Bagel, the Pessimist Sees the Hole*

Alexandra Stoddard, *Grace Notes: A Book of Daily Meditations*, Avon, 1994

Iyanla Vanzant, *Acts of Faith: Daily Meditation for People of Color*, Fireside, 1993

Dr. David Viscott, *Emotional Resistance: Simple Truths for Dealing with the Unfinished Business of Your Past*, Crown, 1997

J. Donald Walters, *Secrets of Inner Peace*, Crystal Clarity, 1992

Zig Ziglar, *Over The Top*, Thomas Nelson, 1998

Go For the Gold: Thoughts on Achieving Your Personal Best, Andrews McMeel, 1995

Quotable Women: A Collections of Shared Thoughts, Running Press, 1994

Random Acts of Kindness, Conari Press, 1993

Women's Wit and Wisdom, Running Press, 1991

PHOTOGRAPHY CREDITS

*A*ll of the photographs are from Joan Lunden's personal collection, except for those listed here.

CHAPTER 1   p x: New Life Entertainment, Inc./Simon Bruty, p 12: Andrew Eccles/ABC, p 15: On-Site Networks, p 19: Larry Busacca Photography, p 21: New Life Entertainment, Inc./In Sync Photography Ltd.

CHAPTER 2   p 24: Brian Fitzgerald/ABC, p 25: Steve Greene/Chicago Cubs, p 28: Ida Mae Astute/ABC, p 31: New Life Entertainment, Inc./Simon Bruty

CHAPTER 3   p 43: Chris Aduama, p 45: Brian Fitzgerald/ABC

CHAPTER 1   p 70: Fred Watkins/ABC

CHAPTER 5   p 84: New Life Entertainment, Inc./Simon Bruty, p 91: KCRA-TV, p 92: Steve Fenn/ABC, p 94: Steve Fenn/ABC, p 95: Larry Busacca Photography

CHAPTER 6   p 112: New Life Entertainment, Inc./Simon Bruty

CHAPTER 7   p 130: Brian Luke Seaward, p 138 Ellen Rogers/Coffee Pond Productions

CHAPTER 8   p 146: New Life Entertainment, Inc./In Sync Photography Ltd., p 159: New Life Entertainment, Inc./In Sync Photography Ltd., p 160: New Life Entertainment, Inc./In Sync Photography Ltd., p 161: New Life Entertainment, Inc./In Sync Photography Ltd., p 162: New Life Entertainment, Inc./In Sync Photography Ltd., p 163: Larry Busacca Photography, p 169: Terry Gruber, p 173: Bruce Taloman/ABC, p 178: Sarah Merions & Co., Inc., p 179: Horsedaily.com/Phelps Photo

CHAPTER 9   p 184: New Life Entertainment, Inc./Simon Bruty, p 190: Sarah Merions & Co., Inc., p 191 (top left): Mark Elkins, p 191 (bottom right): Ida Mae Astute/ABC, p 192: New Life Entertainment, Inc./Simon Bruty, p 194: Donna Svennevik/ABC, p 195 (top): New Life Entertainment, Inc./Simon Bruty, p 195 (bottom): New Life Entertainment, Inc./Simon Bruty, p 197: Brian Luke Seaward, p 201: New Life Entertainment, Inc./Simon Bruty, p 203: Andrew Eccles, p 204: ©1995 FPG International/Richard Prince, p 205: New Life Entertainment, Inc./Simon Bruty

CHAPTER 10   p 208: New Life Entertainment, Inc./Simon Bruty, p 209: Larry Busacca Photography; Michael Krauss Productions, p 211: Cathy Blaivas/ABC

OTHER CREDITS   Design: Arlene Lee, Mighty Dimension, Inc., Illustrations p 90, 128, 136, 214: Anthony Bari, Digital scans: Command P